LEARNING CLIMATE ENVIRONMENT HOW INFLUENCES HUMAN BEHAVIORS

JOHN LOK

Contents

Preface

Introduction

Behavioral economy is one useful and fun social subject. Behavioral economists ususally research how and why human behaviors may influence economy growth or recession, or how and why economy environment changing factor may influence human behavior changes.

Nowadays, climate changing challenge brings any kinds of negative influences to impact human's life, e.g. natural disasters; food shortages, due to no rain to help farmers to grow any food, fruit, vegetable etc. or who have no enough foods to feed to provide cows, pigs, sheeps etc. human eaten animals to eat to cause they can not alive in bad climate environment to cause their bodies are thin or unhealth to provide poor quality of meats to human to eat. What climate change can bring social positive and negative influences?

In climate change part, I concentrate on researching whether it has relationship between climate changing and population immigration as well as whether it has relationship between climate changing and business development to any bad climate countries which are caused by climate changing influences. I shall give my opinions to explain whether climate changing will have cause and effect relationship between climate changing countries immigration and poor business development. It is suitable to any readers who have interest to pursue to investigate whether climate changing challenge will bring negative impact to influence large amount of immigration to cause poor business development in bad climate countries. In this book final chapter, I shall indicate evidences to indicate whether climate change factor will be main factor to influence migrant number rising in the future.

In AI part, I shall explain how artificial intelligence had been developed to be applied to any service , working aspects, e.g. auto-driven cars. In the future, it may replace manual transport drivers in possible, e.g. non-manual driven tram, train, bus, taxi etc. public transport service. In factory warehouse environment, it can replace some workers to deliver any goods in warehouse. In shopping center service environment, it can replace security to do patrol jobs. In restaurant, it can replace waiter to deliver food to client's table. So, AI will assist or replace any service workers to do any kinds of simple jobs in any working environment in possible future.

In my this book, I shall concenrate on discussing whether artificial intelligence can bring what advantages or disadvantages to any kinds of office environment. How can they assist office workers' tasks ? Can robotic bring efficiency to office ? Why employers need artificial intelligence either assist or replace any office workers' tasks? Can AI only bring advantages to office working environment ? I shall indicate different kinds of industry office environment whether AI can bring only advantages or advantages and disadvantages to any kinds of office working envirnments. Readers can have more clear understanding whether AI is real suitable technologic tool to assist any office workers' tasks. This book aims to let readers can understand whether how andy why climate change can influence our living. I shall explain how and why climate change can influence social aspect, economic aspect, business aspect, culture aspect and consumer behavioral aspect to our societies. Readers can have more clear understanding how ansy why climate change can have direct or indirect relationship to influence our future social change.

Prologue

will replace human worker more or
assist human worker more
Reference
5.4 How can (AI) influence labor market?
● How can human society job nature
to be changed to artificial intelligent society?
● Why does human need artificial intelligence machines?
● Why does human need artificial intelligence machines?
● How does artificial intelligence influence future working changing in
automation employment and
productivity aspects?

● Is artificial intelligence possible
to replace labor ?
● Can (AI) technology replace human
labour nature of work?
● Why can artificial intelligence satisfy
human needs?
● Is artificial intelligence one good choice
for human future technological benefit?
● How can artificial intelligence impact on workplace?
What is the relationship between (AI) and (CRM)?
● Can (AI) technology impact on customer relationship management (CRM)
?
● How does (AI) technology influence
the future of employment change?
● Can artificial intelligence impact
global office productive efficiency ?
● Can AI help offices to reduce labor number
Artificial intelligent office create what benefits
● what is artificial intelligent technological office
● Why does AI help offices to save energy ? p.120-130
● On Artificial Intelligence In The Workplace: How AI Is Transforming
Your Employee Experience Benefit Aspect
● Surveillance in the workplace
● Workplace Robots

Chapter 6
Learning human behaviors bring what economic influences

ONE

CLIMATE CHANGE HOW INFLUENCES SOCIETY AND CULTURE

● How climate impacts different groups to adapt to live in our society?
Society today may be more vulnerable to global-scale, long-term, climate change than ever before. Even without any human influence, past records show that climate can be expected to continue to undergo considerable change over decades to centuries. Measures for adaption and mitigation will call for policy decisions based on a sound scientific foundation. Better understanding and prediction of climate variations can be achieved most efficiently through a nationally recognized "dec-cen" science plan.
Climate change presents perhaps the most profound challenge ever to have confronted human social, political, and economic systems. The stakes are massive, the risks and uncertainties severe, the economics controversial, the science besieged, the politics bitter and complicated, the psychology puzzling, the impacts devastating, the interactions with other environmental and non-environmental issues running in many directions. This article summarizes the entire work which brings together a representation of the best scholars on climate change and society. It introduces the key topics, themes, layers, and issues related to climate change. It concludes with a discussion of the structure of the book. It begins with the science that first identified climate change as a problem, and how it is received by and in society and government.
Climate change presents perhaps the most profound challenge ever to have

confronted human social, political, and economic systems. The stakes are massive, the risks and uncertainties severe, the economics controversial, the science besieged, the politics bitter and complicated, the psychology puzzling, the impacts devastating, the interactions with other environmental and non-environmental issues running in many directions. The social problem-solving mechanisms we currently possess were not designed, and have not evolved, to cope with anything like an interlinked set of problems of this severity, scale, and complexity. There are no precedents. So far, we have failed to address the challenge adequately. Problems will continue to manifest themselves—both as we try to prevent and as we try to adapt to the consequences of climate change—so human systems will have to learn how better to respond. One of the central social, political, and economic questions of the century is: how then do we act?

As a society, we have structured our day-to-day lives around historical and current climate conditions. We are accustomed to a normal range of conditions and may be sensitive to extremes that fall outside of this range. Climate change could affect our society through impacts on a number of different social, cultural, and natural resources. For example, climate change could affect human health, infrastructure, and transportation systems, as well as energy, food, and water supplies. However, some groups of people will likely face greater challenges than others. Climate change may especially impact people who live in areas that are vulnerable to coastal storms, drought, and sea level rise or people who live in poverty, older adults, and immigrant communities. Similarly, some types of professions and industries may face considerable challenges from climate change. Professions that are closely linked to weather and climate, such as outdoor tourism, commerce, and agriculture, will likely be especially affected.

Different groups have different abilities to cope with climate change impacts. People who live in poverty may have a difficult time coping with changes. These people have limited financial resources to cope with heat, relocate or evacuate, or respond to increases in the cost of food. For example, older adults may be among the least able to cope with impacts of climate change. Elderly person with facial hair wiping his brow, presumably in heat distressElderly people are particularly prone to heat stress. Young children are another sensitive age group, since their immune system and other bodily systems are still developing and they rely on others to care for them in disaster situations.

● The positive and negative relationship between climate change and society

While the effects of climate change—floods, drought, heat stress, species loss, and ecological change—can be experienced very directly, their conceptualization as connected phenomena with common causes is due to climate science, which therefore plays a very basic part when it comes to climate change and society. Natural scientists (such as Steffen in his chapter) tell us that there is now consensus in the climate science community about the reality of climate change, and near consensus on its severity and the broad range of attendant harms and risks. But that consensus does not of course mean the science is then accepted as the basis for policy. Climate science does not provide certain future projections of risks and damages. The projections are entangled in assumptions about how human systems respond over time—as well as natural ones. Climate is an outcome of a complex geo-atmospheric-ecological system, and complex systems always have a capacity to surprise by behaving in unanticipated ways. Climate change, furthermore, is only one of a range of interacting phenomena of global environmental change caused or affected by human activity. We may indeed be entering the unknown territory of an 'anthropocene' era where people drive truly major changes in global systems.

● How Climate Change Is Affecting Our Lives

Climate change influences that we considerate health. Climate action is just what the doctor ordered. And we mean that quite literally. Medical professionals have increasingly been sounding the alarm about the risks and consequences of continually burning fossil fuels. Here's the problem. The same dirty fossil fuel emissions that contribute to the greenhouse effect can lead to respiratory diseases – such as asthma – in children and adults. And they can be quite dangerous. Air pollution kills an estimated 7 million people worldwide every year, according to the World Health Organization. By trapping heat into our planet, carbon emissions also damage the human body and mind in other ways. We've all heard about the risks of heat strokes. But did you know that warmer temperatures are linked to a 2 percent increase in mental health issues such as stress, anxiety, and even PTSD?

Climate change influences that we considerate where our home location choice. There's really no place like home. But for many living in coastal communities, sea-level rise could lead to an unwanted (and sudden) move. As our globe warms, glaciers melt and ocean water expands, leading seas to rise about 7 to 8 inches on average since 1900 – about 3 inches of that since 1993. The added volume of water creeping up coastlines slowly swallows land and homes and fuels more flooding inland (to name just a few impacts). For example, in the United States, from 2005 to 2015, the median annual number of flood days more than doubled on the East Coast between Florida and North Carolina, thanks in part to rising sea levels. In Miami, even residents that live far away from the beach could be forced to relocate. Lower-income, people of color, and immigrants could lose their homes to wealthy residents who want to move away from the coast and into neighborhoods safe from the water, driving property values and rents up and out of reach of regular people. This is called "climate gentrification," and it's a hot topic within the environmental justice movement.

Also, climate change influences we considerate what health food that we choose to eat. No two people in this world are exactly the same. But there's something that we all do, regardless of our culture, language, or personality. We all eat. So it's hard to ignore the impacts of climate change on food. The same CO2 accumulating in our atmosphere thanks to fossil fuels is actually changing the composition of fruits and vegetables that we eat, making them less nutritious. Extra CO2 is speeding up photosynthesis and causing plants to grow with more sugar and less calcium, protein, zinc, and important vitamins. According to Harvard researchers, if we don't reduce carbon emissions right now, this could spell big problem for our diets. By the middle of the century about 175 million more people could develop a zinc deficiency and 122 million people could become protein deficient as a result of these changes to plant physiology.

Climate change how influences culture

● How culture influences people's response to climate change

How people choose to consume resources and use contraception influences their responses to climate change, according to a team of psychologists. Some behaviors offset environmental gains. If a family buys a fuel-efficient vehicle but chooses to drive more miles than they previously did, there is no gain for the environment. Also, while the average U.S. household size is decreasing, Americans are generally choosing to live in larger homes, counteracmade in smaller spaces.

Decisions about environmental consumption and behaviors that use environmental resources are influenced by culture as well as an individual's abilities and motivations, the researchers noted. Some cultural factors are structural. For example, as people began moving further away from city centers, cars became important for transportation. Other cultural factors, however, influence perceived needs and desires. The types of cars people drive and how fast people drive influence how much gasoline is consumed. People's cars and speed are often both influenced by advertising and others' purchasing and driving behaviors.ade in smaller spaces.

People adjust their explanations for behaviors in ways that allow them to maintain their consumer lifestyles. Carpool lanes decrease carbon dioxide emissions and lower costs of commuting. In one study on carpooler explanations for driving choices, the researchers noted that prior to the existence of carpool lanes commuters said carpooling was too expensive. After carpool lanes were available, commuters were surveyed again and reported that flexibility prevented them from carpooling. Cultural and individual abilities and needs also influence contraceptive use. Population growth in India has in part been attributed to the importance placed on male children, creating a cultural need to have more children in order to increase the number of sons.

● How could a changing climate affect human fertility?

Human adaptation to climate change may include changes in fertility, according to a new study. They found that, through its economic effects, climate change could have a substantial impact on fertility, as people decide how much time and money they devote to child-rearing, and whether to use those resources to have more children or invest more in the future of each child. Climate scientists found that, through its economic effects, climate change could have a substantial impact on fertility, as people decide how much time and money they devote to child-rearing, and whether to use those resources to have more children or invest more in the future of each child. They used a quantitative model that combined standard economic-demographic theory with existing estimate of the economic consequences of climate change. The model examined two example economies, Colombia and Switzerland. It focused on how the demographic impacts of climate change might differ across locations and between richer and poorer countries.The team's model follows individuals through two stages of life, childhood and adulthood. In the model, parents must decide how to divide limited resources between supporting current family consumption, having children, and paying for each child's education. Children's future income depends on parental decisions.

Increases in global temperature affect agricultural and non-agricultural sectors differently. Near the equator, where many poorer countries are, climate change has a larger negative effect on agriculture.This leads to scarcity of agricultural goods, higher agricultural prices and wages and ultimately, a labour reallocation. Because agriculture makes less use of skilled labour, our model showed that climate change decreases the return on acquiring skills, leading parents to invest fewer resources in the education of each child, and to increase fertility.

TWO

CLIMATE CHANGE HOW INFLUENCES ECONOMY AND BUSINESS

● How Climate Change Impacts the Economy?

What do scientific findings mean in human terms? An answer is given by economics, which can attach cost estimates to the current impacts and projections of future impacts of climate change. Warmer temperatures, sea level rise and extreme weather will damage property and critical infrastructure, impact human health and productivity, and negatively affect sectors such as agriculture, forestry, fisheries and tourism. The demand for energy will increase as power generation becomes less reliable, and water supplies will be stressed. Damage to other countries around the globe will also affect U.S. business through disruption in trade and supply chains.

Low estimates, with costs concentrated among the rural poor in developing countries. A recent climate scientist report examined how climate change could affect 22 different sectors of the economy under two different scenarios: if global temperatures rose 2.8° C from pre-industrial levels by 2100, and if they increased by 4.5° C. The study projected that if the higher-temperature scenario prevails, climate change impacts on these 22 sectors could cost the U.S. $520 billion each year. If we can keep to 2.8° C, it would cost $224 billion less. In any case, the U.S. stands to suffer large economic losses due to climate change, second only to India, according to another study. "For example, it's not just whether a building is underwater or not," he said. "What's important are the harder-to-define things like when does societal risk perception shift? It may be that buildings lose their value before the water actually arrives, once people realize that eventually the water's going to arrive. We need deeper thinking about the interconnection between physical and social systems." Hence, climate change will damafe buildinf , due to a building is caused to damage by poor climate underwater attack. (Jeremy Martinich & Allison Crimmins) 2019.

In addition to flooding, increased heat and drought will likely reduce crop yields. According to a 2011 National Academy of Sciences report, for every degree Celsius the global thermostat rises, there will be a 5 to 15 percent decrease in overall crop production. Many commodity crops such as corn, soybean, wheat, rice, cotton, and oats do not grow well above certain temperature thresholds. In addition, crops will be affected by less availability of water and groundwater, increased pests and weeds, and fire risk. And as farmers struggle to stay afloat by finding ways to adapt to changing conditions, prices will likely increase and be passed along to consumers. Moreover, Much of our society's critical infrastructure is at risk from flooding. "Sea level rise could potentially cause a loss of value of assets in the trillions of dollars—probably anywhere from two to five trillion dollars—by the end of the century," said Heal. "That's loss from damage to housing, damage to airports on the coasts, damage to docks, the railway line that runs up and down the East Coast all of which is within a few feet of sea level, damage to I-95 which runs also along the coast. And that's just the East Coast. If you take a global perspective, this is repeated around the world." Much of this infrastructure will likely need to be repaired or replaced. Military bases are also vulnerable. According to a 2016 report published by the Center for Climate and Security policy institute, sea level rise could flood parts of military bases along the East and Gulf coasts for up to three months a year as soon as 2050. Inland military installations near rivers are also vulnerable, because they can overflow with heavy precipitation, which is expected to become more common as the atmosphere warms. Extreme weather will necessitate more maintenance and repair for runways and roads, infrastructure and equipment. (Jeremy Martinich & Allison Crimmins) 2019.

Hence, once we get past controversies over cost estimates and distributions, economics also provides a powerful set of analytics for thinking about the choice of policy instruments to achieve the desired level of mitigation (expressed in terms of targets and timetables for total greenhouse gas emissions).The consensus among economists—at least those steeped in the neoclassical paradigm that dominates the discipline—is that market-based instruments are the most efficient, and in particular emissions trading or cap-and-trade.Emissions trading requires that some authority sets a cap on total emissions, then issues permits for quantities that add up to that cap. These permits can then be traded, such that companies for which reducing pollution is expensive can buy permits from those for which reductions are cheaper. The economic theory is very clear, but the politics and policy making is much murkier. Even before we get to monitoring and compliance, polluters with sufficient political power will demand exemptions and/or free permits for themselves. So when emissions trading schemes are proposed or introduced, it is common to find whole economic sectors exempted (for example, agriculture in Australia), or established dirty industries (for example, coal-burning electricity generators) favored at the expense of more efficient but less established competitors.

Finally, national governments are embedded in market economies that constrain what they can do, and the social realm is often limited by economistic frames and discourse. However, markets are not necessarily just a source of constraint. Markets are made up of producers and consumers who might themselves change their behavior in ways that reduce emissions. The most important producers here are large corporations. Why might they change their ways? In part, if they thought the world was moving in a low-carbon direction (whether by choice or necessity), positioning themselves to take advantage of this shift might be profitable. Of course this positioning would need to be more than the kind of rhetoric that enabled (for example) BP to market itself as 'Beyond Petroleum'—at least until an oil spill in the Gulf of Mexico in 2010 exposed a range of problems in its public relations approach (in addition to its safety practices). While there may be money to be made in producing goods for a low-greenhouse gas economy, the problem is that currently there is much more money to be made in climate-unfriendly activities. Corporate responses to the challenge of climate change have been highly variable , and there is little reason to suppose a significant number of corporations will play a leadership role if governments do not. The only corporations that do have a clear financial incentive to take the risks of climate change very seriously are insurance companies. This is especially true of the big reinsurance companies with potentially high exposure to damages caused by extreme weather events.

On conclusion , a decarbonizing economy would of course have to involve changes in patterns of consumption, whether induced by government policy and price increases, or chosen by consumers through changing mores. Such basic individual and broad cultural changes that affect consumption have been promoted by a variety of social movements, religious actors, and celebrities. Many environmental organizations focus on consumer behavior—from the individual level up to the decarbonization and transition of towns and regions—both as a source of direct change and as a clear economic and political statement. The 'green governmentality' identified by Lipschutz and McKendry in their chapter would help mold citizens of a new ecological order, whose consumption demands could look quite different from those characteristic of industrial society. However, consumption choices are limited by the social-economic structure, which conditions the range of easy options that individual consumers have. Luke also insists we understand the dangers of such forms of such behavioral control, even if it does look green. At any rate, changing consumer habits are no substitute for coordinated collective action.

A person engaged in a certain activity does not think about the consequences, which soon become global. Scientists around the world are trying to fight warming in every possible way. Various conferences, meetings, experiments, methods of opposition and climate mitigation are organized. But the correct answers have not yet been found.

According to scientists ' calculations, the warming will last until 2050,and later the cooling will begin. Then , they predict how climate change can impact to our future economic to be worse. The reasons are as below:

Impacts of climate change today:

- Due to global warming and climate change, the territory of deserts and semi-deserts in Africa is expanding;

- the melting of glaciers leads to the mass death of polar animals, for example, polar bears have long been included in the Red book;

- due to rising sea levels, many people may lose their habitat (Venice, Maldives, Seychelles and other small Islands);

- due to climate change, the drought will become even more severe, which can adversely affect crop yields in the African and Asian regions.

The global cooling is still being discussed only within the framework of a hypothesis. Questions are raised about the relationship between warming and cyclical glaciation. After warming, cooling and possibly even glaciation will begin. Some geologists also agree with this hypothesis. Especially since the Earth as a whole is gradually cooling down.This is proved by certain minerals, such as Olivine, which were previously formed at very high temperatures. Now the formation of Olivine does not occur, which means that the subsurface temperatures are falling.

Effects:

- increased snow cover, which will lead to even more cooling. Why? Snow cover has a powerful reflectivity, that is, solar energy will not heat the earth's surface, but will be reflected from it;
- mass extinction of animals, adaptation of some of them and modification of the organism;
- perhaps the glaciers will cover a larger area than before. But according to forecasts, only the North of Russia, Scandinavia, and Canada will be affected.

All of above countries weather will be influenced to be worse and their economic will be influened worse also. So, climate change may bring future some countries to encounter worse economic effect.

reference

Jeremy Martinich & Allison Crimmins ,(08, April, 2019). Climate damages and adaptation potential across diverse sectors of the United StatesNature Climate Change .volume 9, pages397–404(2019) source: https://www.nature.com/articles/s41558-019-0444-6

Climate change how influences business

● Why does climate change influence business building damage

With climate changes seemingly impacting many areas of the United States, water usage is a new consideration for areas that formerly had no water shortages. Droughts in various areas of the country force organizations and individuals to reconsider how they waste water and mandate cutbacks.Creative innovations are needed to make these rapid and dramatic reductions possible for most organizations.Resource conservation is another area with major potential for savings within existing buildings. So, climate change can bring negative influence to damage any properties, such as offices will be easily to be damaged, consequently, it will bring high repair expenditure to any businessmen. I shall expalin as below:

The initial focus of most industry sustainability guidelines began with construction of new buildings. The ability to influence sustainable outcomes is most easily identified by contrasting a traditional building, or one built without consideration of integrated systemsand savings, with a new, highly integrated, high-performance structure. The design and commissioning provides great momentum for the sustainability movement as more and more organizations become familiar with the USGBC's Leadership in Energy and Environmental Design (LEED) guidelines and the need to improve our total life-cycle costs through design, construction, the long operational period, and final disposal. Acceptance of new building improvements has been well embraced.

Sustainability Applied to Existing Buildings Operations Of primary interest to facility managers is the ability to support the organization and provide high-performance spaces for accomplishing organizational objectives. Reduction of energy usage is the most visible, and most easily documented, feature of sustainable building systems. With energy costs soaring, mandates to dramatically reduce energy usage are widespread worldwide. Facility managers are ordered to keep cost escalations within sometimes unrealistic ranges, and are also charged with continuing to keep the organization and its workers comfortable and productive in their workspaces. All of above property damage cost will be caused by global bad climate change influences.

● How businessmen act to fight climate change ?

There is a risk that as the immediate crisis wanes and its economic consequences become clearer, we cast aside longer-term aspirations in pursuit of short-term easy fixes, many of which would have adverse environmental consequences. These include rolling back environmental standards, stimulating the economy by subsidising fossil-fuel-heavy industries and focusing on making more things, rather than using them better. Hence, it bring this question due to climate change can bring negative influence to businesses, how businessmen act to fight climate change ? Business action on climate change includes a range of activities relating to global warming, and to influencing political decisions on global-warming-related regulation, such as the Kyoto Protocol. Major multinationals have played and to some extent continue to play a significant role in the politics of global warming, especially in the United States, through lobbying of government and funding of global warming deniers. Business also plays a key role in the mitigation of global warming, through decisions to invest in researching and implementing new energy technologies and energy efficiency measures. (See also individual and political action on climate change.)

What is the impact of climate change on business?

There are multiple impacts of climate change on companies. On the one hand, it creates a series of new business risks. Besides the most obvious physical risks (for example, the operational impacts of extreme weather events, or supply shortages caused by water scarcity), companies are exposed to transition risks which arise from society's response to climate change, such as changes in technologies, markets and regulation that can increase business costs, undermine the viability of existing products or services, or affect asset values. Another climate-related risk for companies is the potential liability for emitting greenhouse gases (GHG).

An increasing number of legal cases have been brought directly against fossil fuel companies and utilities in recent years, holding them accountable for the damaging effects of climate change.

But climate change also offers business opportunities. Firstly, companies can aim to improve their resource productivity (for example by increasing energy efficiency), thereby reducing their costs. Secondly, climate change can spur innovation, inspiring new products and services which are less carbon intensive or which enable carbon reduction by others. Thirdly, companies can enhance the resilience of their supply chains, for example by reducing reliance on price-volatile fossil fuels by shifting towards renewable energy. Together, these actions can foster competitiveness and unlock new market opportunities.

Do companies feel the pressure to act on climate change?

To gain a better understanding of how companies perceive the issue of climate change, the latest edition of the European CFO survey asked close to 1,200 financial executives across Europe to what extent their companies are feeling the pressure to act and what precisely they are doing.10 The survey shows that most companies are feeling the pressure from various stakeholders. Clients and customers are most often named as sources of significant pressure, but employees, regulators, civil society and investors are not far behind

The degree to which companies are feeling external pressure varies greatly. About 30 per cent do not perceive significant pressure from anyone, while for 19 per cent the pressure comes from only one or two stakeholders – usually from regulators and civil society. Larger companies (defined as those with annual revenues of €1 billion or more) are more likely to feel the pressure from several sides, with almost two-thirds (61 per cent) of CFOs reporting that they feel the pressure to act from three or more stakeholders and almost 70 per cent feeling under pressure from clients. By contrast, the regulator is the main source of pressure on smaller companies (that is, with annual revenues of up to €100 million).

The pressure felt from different stakeholders also varies across industries. In tourism, automotive, consumer goods and energy and utilities, the share of executives reporting pressure to act is among the highest for each stakeholder group. There are some differences between these sectors, however, in the degree of influence coming from the various stakeholders. For example, in tourism, consumer goods and automotive, pressure from clients is felt more strongly. In energy and utilities the pressure comes more from investors and regulators .

● Why does climate is the biggest risk to business (and the world)?
Nowadays, many companies and investors are waking up to the dangers posed by climate change and extreme weather. Many now consider environmental risks, such as droughts and wildfires, to be even more dangerous than turbulent markets. Top investors are demanding that more companies draw up environmental action plans. They're also asking CEOs to consider risks to their business caused by shifting consumer attitudes toward climate change. Many climate scientist their view of risks tends to be dominated by the short-term horizon, and climate is still seen as more long-term than geopolitical risk ... but that report has started to pull more focus on long term business climate risk.
 ● How firms adapt climate change ?
From the early days of seafaring trade, dealing with the weather has been an integral part of doing business. Today, however, concerns over climate change are taking this to a whole new level, and companies will have to adapt to growing regulatory, environmental, and consumer pressures. But delay is not a strategy. Organizations can benefit by taking action to recognize and even anticipate such climate-related risks as changing government policies, product-preference shifts, and price volatility. The climate risk to organizations may include as below:
Firstly, it is physical risks are those related to damage inflicted on infrastructure and other assets, such as factories and supply-chain operations, by the increased frequency and intensity of extreme weather events, such as wildfires, floods, or hurricanes. According to the New England Journal of Medicine, the frequency and severity of climate-related

disasters like floods, droughts, and storm surges has increased markedly since the 1970s.

This can affect company performance in real and visible ways. In 2012, for example, Cargill, one of the world's largest food and agricultural companies, posted its worst quarterly earnings in two decades, in large part because of the US drought. While no single event can be attributed to climate change, of course, this is an example of how climate can and does affect business prospects. Western Digital Technologies, a major supplier of hard disk drives, posted a sharp decline in revenues in 2011 after flooding in Thailand, where most of its production was located. That loss of production meant global supply slumped, with severe reverberations for computer manufacturers.

Such physical risks are impossible to control, but companies can take steps to prepare for the changes that could occur in years and decades to come. First, it helps to forecast a range of reasonable scenarios; doing so may require the help of specialized climate modelers. Climate forecasting can highlight high-level risk probabilities by region, such as for flood, drought, or sea-level rise, and for long-term changes in such factors as temperature, humidity, or rainfall patterns. The scenarios should help reveal which parts of the business are vulnerable. A variety of mitigating risk processes, technical standards, and capabilities can then be put in place. In the long term, risk management could call for changes to supply chains (to build in geographic variability or redundancy), including moving away from suppliers and/or locations that are highly exposed.

Secondly, it is price risks refer to the increased price volatility of raw materials and other commodities. Drought can raise the price of water; climate-related regulation can drive up the cost of energy. High-tech and renewable-energy industries, for example, face price risks in the competition for rare earths, which are used in the production of computer hard drives, televisions, wind turbines, solar photovoltaic systems, and electric vehicles. For more than a decade, the prices of many resources have been both rising and volatile. An unstable climate could ratchet up the pressure further, forcing companies to cope with uncertainty around inputs to production, energy, transport, and insurance. Some companies are taking significant steps to get ahead of this concern. IKEA is in the process of substituting renewables for conventional sources of energy; in time, it hopes to be largely self-sufficient with regard to power. In that event, the retailer will have a good idea of what price it will pay for power and will insulate itself against global and regional energy price spikes.Volkswagen is doing something similar. To hedge against the possibility of rising fossil-fuel prices, the German car maker is investing €1 billion in renewable-energy projects and is aiming to power its manufacturing sites mainly through on-site production. These are just two examples: we expect more and more companies to go "off grid" for both strategic and economic reasons.

Thirdly, it is product risks refer to core products becoming unpopular or even unsellable. Effects could range from losing a little market share to going under entirely. Alternative cooling technologies, for example, could conceivably displace air-conditioning systems; ski resorts that no longer can count on snow or cold weather could go under. Regulatory and production costs could raise the price of coal in some markets above that of lower-carbon competition, with ripple effects for mining-equipment manufacturers and related industries.This kind of risk, of course, is familiar; new products, by definition, displace older ones. The difference is that responding to climate-related pressures can change the entire context in which a business operates, not just a specific segment. It's more like the change from the horse-and-buggy era to the car than shifting from manual to automatic transmission. Utilities, for one, know this; they are seeing their traditional business model threatened in markets where renewable energy accounts for a greater part of new generation.

On the positive side, however, greener products are emerging in a number of industries. The construction and infrastructure sectors are developing new products and services that cater to cleaner cities, such as electric-vehicle charging infrastructure, renewables integration, smart metering, smart grids, congestion-fee systems, and high-performance building technologies. In the business-to-consumer sectors, especially retail and consumer products, new segments are making inroads as people make it clear they are willing to pay for greener products. Groceries advertised as sustainable, for example, are growing fast in the United States, and the organic-food sector has seen double-digit growth for the past decade. This is a testament to the emergence of a significant cohort of customers for whom environmental consciousness is a factor in where and what they buy.

How can companies adapt? One approach is to adopt a "design to sustainability" approach, in which new products are designed to minimize waste and to be broken down for reuse or recycling. Another is to redefine corporate strategy to align business interests with climate-change mitigation and adaptation. Siemens, for instance, has developed a dedicated "environmental portfolio" of carbon-efficient products, while Saint-Gobain, the construction and packaging giant, puts sustainable housing technologies at the core of its product-development strategy.

What is External-stakeholder risks ? We define ratings risk as the possibility of higher costs of capital because of climate-related exposure such as carbon pricing, supply-chain disruption, or product obsolescence. While the ratings risk varies widely between and within industries, even companies with carbon-intensive activities can start to manage it. Would you like to learn more about our Sustainability & Resource Productivity Practice?

Foutrhly, it is regulation risk refers to government action prompted by climate change. This can take many forms, including rules that add costs or impede specific business activities, subsidies in support of a competitor, or withdrawal of subsidies. In many industries, government plays a crucial role in setting the rules of the game; with climate change in mind, many of those rules are changing. Around the world, we are seeing governments respond to the possibility of climate change in ways that necessarily affect business prospects. To cite just a few examples: China is launching carbon-trading programs in seven regions in preparation for a potential national plan by 2020. Most US states have introduced renewable portfolio standards, which require a certain proportion of the state's electricity to be produced from renewable sources. Ethiopia has charted a course to become a middle-income country through low-emissions growth with its Climate-Resilient Green Economy strategy.

However, one complication is that on the national and international level, climate-change policies often change, sometimes with the speed of an election result. That makes it difficult for businesses to make long-term investment and operating decisions. Businesses can, however, take the initiative in managing regulation risk. The first step in preparing for and helping to shape future regulation is to understand the policy options. The second step is to develop an internal strategy on climate change to put the company in a position to react effectively to regulations and policy changes. The final step is to work with external stakeholders, such as regulators and industry groups, to get their perspectives.

Fifthly, reputation risk can be either direct, stemming from a company-specific action or policy, or indirect, in the form of public perception of the overall industry. In the climate-change context, reputation risk can be understood as the probability of profitability loss following a business's activities or positions that the public considers harmful. A poor reputation on climate can hurt sales through consumer boycotts or local community protests. It could damage the regulatory environment and investor relationships. And it could make the company less attractive to current or future employees. This is part of a larger trend: the changing expectations of stakeholders. Investors are asking for disclosure of carbon emissions and starting to lodge concerns about "stranded" assets—those that become unusable due to climate-policy regulation or physical climate change. Many employees want sustainability to be part of the day-to-day operations of their companies. Nongovernmental organizations are getting more prominence when it comes to their ability to measure and compare corporate actions. In response, some companies have taken very public steps to adopt climate-change strategies. Unilever, for example, leads the FTSE CDP Carbon Strategy risk and performance index and has improved its carbon efficiency by 40 percent since 1995. Its stated goal is to reduce the carbon and water footprints of its products to half of 2010 levels by 2020. The retailer Kohl's has been recognized for its efforts to green its operations and reduce emissions. IBM has also gotten positive attention for its actions on climate, such as setting rigorous greenhouse-gas-emission standards for suppliers. IBM won a 2013 Climate Leadership Award from the US Environmental Protection Agency for supply-chain leadership and was also recognized in 2014 for its greenhouse-gas management. Just about every company in the Fortune 500 touts its commitment to sustainability. There is still a long way to go in many respects, but it can be said that action has well and truly started.

On conclusion, businesses are re-directing their production lines to provide medical and hygiene supplies, offering free access to their online platforms and supporting their employees in a number of ways, such as increasing their wages, highlighting how agile they can be in responding to critical needs. And governments are committing trillions to help those affected by coronavirus, in what looks like a "race to the top" in providing the most comprehensive support to their citizens.All this shows that a large-scale response to a global crisis is possible. We need to harness this wave of compassion and proactivity to protect vulnerable people in all contexts, including those most exposed to climate impacts.

Adaption to climate change for business development

Do any businesses need to adapt to climate change to develop in themselve countries? I believe a changing climate can impact on business in any countries. The challenges include as below:

1. Worse Natural environment challenge

The climate change will cause either temperature changes to fall down or raise up too much to let people feel very cold or very hot. So, if the country's weather is not very hot, but it's temperature rises up to above 30 degree, even above 40 degree for long time suddenly or if the country's weather is not very cold, but its' temperature falls down to 0 degree, even above 0 degree for long time suddenly. Then, I believe the country people will choose to leave their country to immigrate to another suitable weather of country to live long time. Also, climate changing will cause floods, river drier, storms natural disasters to impact some businesses to bring negative environment influences. For example, farming industry, food supply chain, e.g. supermarket retail industry. Moreover, climate changing also brings much cost expenditure to any country governments, e.g. beyong property damages, the floods also impacted the economy and influences the ability of workers to access work, water shortages, impacts on water quality.

2. Labour supply challenge

Thus, in global business environment, climate change will impact global economy. For example, The effect and long run effects of climate change will most certainly be negactive for global economic activity. Damage to the global capital stock and shortage to labour supply will reduce to productivity, due to the worse climate changing environment countries' people will choose to immigrate to the better climate environment countries to cause the worse climate changing environment countries' population to be reduced to bring its labour supply numbers also be decreased. If many young aged high or low educational people chose to leave their countries to immigrate to the better climate countries to live in the long time suddenly. Then, the worse climate countries will lose many labour supply in long time. Although, any manufacturing or service or retail industries will have many jobs to supply, but the labor demand will reduce to cause poor business environment to the bad climate countries.

3. Inflation challenge

Also, inflation will increase as production is cut to be fall down, due to shortage of labor supply challenge brings any manufacturing product supply number is also decreased. Particularly real incomes and spending in the worse climate changing countries. Thus, inflation is likely to rise over time, driven by rising food prices and an increase in the cost of energy.

Although, the climate of some countries is predicted to become more accommodative to agricultural yields in the medium term, but the long-run implications of rising temperature are likely to reduce global crop yields overall. Also, costs are also likely to increase through higher insurance changes. But premiums in climate risk areas are increased, feeding into higher costs for businesses and homeowners. From this perspective, the cost of climate changes are already affecting global activity.

1.1 Scientists' opinions of quantifying the impact on activity

Some scientists gave opinions to indicate that how climate damage functions of quantifying the impact on activity. They showed to value the future loss in economic output attributable to climate change produces a range of estimates which vary according to views about whether a fipping point is reached between 2 to 4 degree warming. In a worst cause scenario, global warming could be seen to reduce annual GDP growth by over 1 % between the present day and 2080 year.

They also predicted developing countries are set to absorb much of the losses caused by climate change. relying more heavily on climate sensitive sectors, such as agriculture and tourism and having naturally warmer climates, they will experience the most adverse effects an activity.

Assessing the impact of climate change is at least, an extremely complex challenge with uncertainty about both the degree of future global warming and the subsequent impact on global activity. There are clearly some benefits as well as costs as the planet warms. There is also the unknown of how technological progree will respond and potentially alter the path of global warming.

However, increasingly awareness of the issue means there is a growing demand for a view shareholders who are either concerned about how the companies they own impact the environment, worried aout the effect of climate change and people immigrate to better climate countries to work and live.

1.2 How Global warming influences economic growth

However, global warming will primarily influence economic growth through damage to property, last productivity, mass migration and security threats. For New York, examples of the economic damage, such extreme weather events can cause such as: rising sea levels will also likely harm economic outputs as businesses become losses.

Climate change is likely reduce the capital stock and productivity in the world economy. If we assume less capital stock is available, due to the damage inflicted from climate change. We would see a fall in the productive capacity of the world economy. This would translate into a downward shift in the world production function as each unit of labour produces less output. Lower labour productivity may not just occur, due to a lower level of capital stock.

However, higher global temperatures may affect food security, promote the spread of infections diseases. Such those migration and global warming factors are likely to cause greater incapacity and social populatin uneven distribution and as a result will reduce both the affectiveness (productivity) and the amount of labour available to produce output.

According to Mendelsohn (2013), indicated the biggest threat change poses to economic growth is from immediate, aggessive and inefficient migration policies. The process of adaptation and migration will require a temporary economic transition from consumption to investment. Part of Africa and Asia most at risk. Some regions in the work include Sub-regions Africa and South and South East Asia. According to the world bank: In South Asia cities, such as Mumbai and Kolkata will face increased floding, warming temperature and intense cyclones loss of snow melt from the Himalayas will also reduce the flow of water into the Indus Ganges and Brahmaputra basins. Vietnam will produce most rises , but flood security will be a major challenge, due to drough and shifts in rainfall.

THREE
CLIMATE CHANGE HOW INFLUENCES CONSUMER BEHAVIOR

● How climate change influences traveller behaviors ?

Reduce tourism's carbon footprint to address the sector's contribution to climate change. Climate change threatens all life on the planet, as well as the very destinations that tourism relies on. From lush tropical islands to snowy mountain peaks, your favorite vacation spots could be at risk. As the planet warms, rising sea levels, extreme weather, and increasing temperatures are impacting ecosystems and communities around the world. Beaches are shrinking, coral reefs are bleaching, and alpine resorts are left snowless and dry. If we want to save our planet and protect these special places, it's up to each and every one of us to reduce our impact.

Tourism is not just a victim of global warming – it also contributes to the problem. Tourism alone is responsible for 8% of the world's carbon emissions. As more and more people travel each year, this footprint is only growing. When we travel, carbon emissions are generated throughout our trips. While flying is the largest source of these emissions, other activities, such as using the AC in hotels or taking a boat ride, produce CO_2 as well. Beyond these direct emissions, tourism development can also cause CO_2 to be released by degrading ecosystems that act as carbon sinks. If actions aren't taken to reduce tourism's carbon footprint and ensure the industry operates more sustainably, the resulting impacts on the environment and human life could be devastating.

For any traveler concerned about timing, safety or cost, the days of being able to simply make reservations and hope for sunny weather are over. Climate change is increasing the frequency and intensity of certain extreme weather events. You can still be a globe-trotter, but these are some tips that can help minimize your travel risk. Hence, climate change influences any travellers how to make trip deicsion, before you book, check your credit cards for travel-related benefits that will cover weather-related events, and use the one that has the best protection to book your trip. Keep in mind that you usually can't cancel a trip just because you see massive clouds on the horizon. To be able to cancel for a full refund, the storm must have already hit your destination and done severe damage, rendering it "uninhabitable." However, an insurance plan can cover prepaid trip costs if weather interrupts your travels or causes delays, baggage loss or missed connections. Finally, purchase insurance in advance, especially during hurricane season. Once a storm has a name and a path, you can no longer buy travel insurance for your trip. Hence, weather predictions have become much more accurate, but they can tell you only so much. The forecasts are particularly good at showing when a big hurricane or snowstorm will hit, but other extreme weather events, such as tornadoes, can be more challenging for forecasters and travelers to anticipate.

In general, travellers can't predict where a tornado is going to happen, but you can predict where they're likely to form. For example, when the jet stream takes a big dip in the middle of the country in the spring, the risk for violent thunderstorms that can unleash damaging winds and hail and delay travel increases. Temperatures are heating up globally, said Francis, and heat waves are lasting longer. Record heat spread throughout Europe in June, even as wildfires blazed in Catalonia. These are the kinds of extreme-weather scenarios we're likely to see more of in the future, It doesn't mean travellers shouldn't go, you just need to pay attention and be ready for your travel to be disrupted because extreme weather is increasing. Hence, climate change will influence travellers ' trip choice.

● Climate change how influences householder behavior

We're looking at a range of actions from household weatherization to changing driving behavior, to changing thermostat settings, to changing purchasing behavior for more efficient appliances and things of that nature. Climate changing may influence householder behavior when the householder needs to make gas or oil choice for cooking , which is the cheapest and fastest way of reducing emissions. For example, that's equivalent to the total emissions of France. It's also equivalent to the combined emissions of the petroleum refining, iron and steel and aluminum industries combined. One of the largest problems that we face is getting over the presumption that people have that individual behavior or household behavior doesn't matter. But when you aggregate it across 300 million individuals and 100 million households, it has a very large impact on total U.S. greenhouse gas emissions.

Would these reductions actually have a palpable effect on the climate over the next decade or so? We don't know precisely where that next contribution of carbon emissions will cause a very substantial change in the climate. But it's a mistake to look at the problem as if any one small piece of it doesn't matter. The problem is significant enough that all the small pieces put together matter. We need to reduce greenhouse gas emissions by somewhere between 50 and 80 percent by 2050. And we won't get there if we slice off each small percentage. However, that's an understandable assumption. But there's actually no research that supports that idea. In fact, the little bit of research that's available suggests that people, when they do something good for the environment, don't do less other good things. And, in fact, there are a number of psychological phenomena that suggests that we might actually induce more support for behavior change. When someone becomes committed to a certain behavior, they're more likely to follow through in other areas as well. So there are a number of reasons why we might assume that if people take small individual steps, it actually contributes to additional support for political change or for governmental change. But the research is very thin on that. And that's an area that we need to do further work on.

● Is climate change important to consumers?

Weather has the biggest influence on consumer behaviour after the economy, according to the British Retail Consortium. It affects consumers' emotional state, drives their purchase decisions, and dictates how much they are willing to spend. The effects are far more pervasive than the obvious examples that spring to mind; ice cream selling on hot days, and umbrellas when it's raining.

In reality, weather affects practically every consumer purchase decision. The food we eat, the clothes we wear, what car we drive and even what type of house we buy, can all be determined by commonplace fluctuations in weather. Understanding this relationship can pay huge dividends for both brands and performance marketers. This data can be leveraged to market products at the most profitable time and in the most impactful way. By executing weather based marketing campaigns, brands can gain a real competitive advantage.As scientists become increasingly convinced that we are living in a new geological epoch, defined by humankind's impact on the planet – the Anthropocene – it seems that the public are increasingly messages around climate change. Even a few years ago, data from the Ipsos Global Trends survey showed that three-quarters of Britons attributed most climate change to human activity, while two-thirds believed the country was headed for an environmental disaster without rapid changes to people's habits. As always, there is a gulf between what people 'say' motivates or concerns them and what actually drives their behaviour.

A new global study by Ipsos (2019), carried out online among adults across 28 countries between February 22 and March 8, 2019, finds that while people worldwide have a myriad of concerns when it comes to environmental issues, climate change has climbed in importance since last year.Polling we conducted to coincide with Earth Day in March 2019 showed 37% of global citizens put climate change as one of the top environmental issues, narrowly ahead of air pollution (35%) and dealing with rubbish and waste (34%). Other issues – whether deforestation (24%), depletion of natural resources (22%) and the overpackaging of consumer goods (15%) – were further behind still.

Effect of Weather on Purchase Method

On the most basic level, weather affects which channels consumers use to make purchases. For instance, during warm and sunny days, bricks and mortar stores often enjoy more footfall, whereas during periods of inclement weather, traffic to online portals can increase. However, much is depended on seasonality, industry and product. This study found that on wet or cold days there was a 12% increase in website traffic for retailers in the home & furniture, wholesale, and clothing verticals - compared to that on warm and sunny days. However, interestingly there was no significant difference for big box retailers. Because weather driven demand varies with industry, it is critical that brands and advertisers have insights on how various weather conditions affect product sales, as well as methods of purchase.

Effect of Weather on Mood

The second way in which weather influences consumer behaviour is through its effect on mood. Studies show that temperature, humidity, air pressure, snow fall, and, especially sunlight can have a huge impact on a consumer's mind frame and by extension their spending. A 2010 study by

Kyle B. Murray revealed that exposure to sunlight dramatically increased levels of consumption as well as the amount spent per item. Experiments show consumers would willingly pay 37% more for green tea and 56% more for gym membership after being exposed to sunlight. Similarly, a study by Persinger and Levesque found that 40% of mood evaluations were accounted for by a combination of meteorological events; in particular, barometric pressure and sunshine. Many retailers are savvy to this phenomenon and use bright halogen lighting which mimics the effect of sunlight in their stores. Consumer mind-frame can also be determined by seasonal weather events – so if there is snowfall in late October then this could get consumers into the Christmas spirit early and therefore boost pre-Christmas sales.

As well as affecting our mood, our propensity to spend, and our preferred channels of purchase, weather is a critical driver of product demand. The food and drinks, pharmaceutical, and fashion industries are most heavily affected by this phenomenon. Luckily, weather-driven demand can be predicted with unerring accuracy - with identifiable trigger points. For instance, if temperatures reach over 18 degrees in the UK, supermarkets know that there will be a 22% increase in fizzy drinks, 20% increase in juices, and 90% increase in garden furniture. Likewise, a 1 degree F drop in temperature in the US can lead to a huge increase in sales of soup, porridge, and lipcare products. Supermarkets leverage weather intelligence on a daily basis to guide stock management decisions – and now advertisers are also beginning to use live weather data as a way of contextualising ad campaigns.

Hence, I believe that climate change, such as extreme cold or hot, this extreme weather will influence consumer purchase behavior has significant change when he/she needs to go to shopping in the extreme hot or cold climate environment. Many environmental organizations focus on consumer behavior—from the individual level up to the decarbonization and transition of towns and regions—both as a source of direct change and as a clear economic and political statement. The 'green governmentality' identified by Lipschutz and McKendry in their chapter would help mold citizens of a new ecological order, whose consumption demands could look quite different from those characteristic of industrial society. However, as consumption choices are limited by the social-economic structure, which conditions the range of easy options that individual consumers have. Luke also insists we understand the dangers of such forms of such behavioral control, even if it does look green. At any rate, changing consumer habits are no substitute for coordinated collective action.

reference
Ipsos, Climate change increases in importance to citizens around the world, 19 April 2019, source; https://www.ipsos.com/ipsos-mori/en-uk/climate-change-increases-importance-citizens-around-world

Climate change how influences global energy need

Global warming and energy shortage challenge

We are facing global warmth and natural resource and energy shortage challenges. Due to our Earth have limited natural resource numbers to supply to us to manufacture energy, but global population has been increasing every year. Thus, it is possible that we have energy shortage crisis. Also, manufactures are spending too much energy to waste to manufacture any products, the energy will cause air or water pollution in manufacturing process or drivers are driving their vehicles to pollute air on the roads. Then it will cause global warmth crisis. How we can avoid these both crises to occur. I shall give some recommendation as below:

Primary energy exploration method

● Greenhouse primary gas energy

Have you ever seen a greenhouse? A greenhouse can trap heat in the sunlight and keeps the air inside the greenhouse warm enough for plants to grow. The glass roof and walls of a greenhouse let in sunlight but prevent heat from escape, this makes the greenhouse warm inside. Similarly, some gases in the Earth's atmosphere can trap heat from the sun and keep the Earth warm. This is called the greenhouse effect. The gases energy that can trap heat from the sun are called greenhouse gases. It is future one kind of potential primary energy to reduce environmental pollution new energy products for human consuming.

● Underwater primary water energy

The world's underwater meeting took place around a table about five meters underwater. Many scientists believe that due to melting of ice caused by global warming, the sea level will rise by as much as 1 m by the end of this century. If the level of the sea rises in the future, most regions of the country will be underwater.

Questions

What impact of global warming is mentioned by underground water?

Can human apply underwater water technology to explore natural underground water energy to avoid global warming threat?

Why do we need to Safety in using fuel and handle gas leaks? Why do we feel town gas smell? How is electricity located at electric station far away from town area? How to solve problems caused by the use of fossil fuels? How to reduce the use of fossil fuels?

To solve the problems, the best way is to reduce our used of fossil fuel. This helps prevent fossil fuels form being used up too quickly. Also, it helps us to reduce environmental problems because fewer pollutants are given out when less fossil fuels are used. Can human help to reduce the use of fossil fuels? Fossil fuels are mainly in power station. Although we use some fossil fuels for our gas cooker and car, it won't make much difference if I use less.

Fossil fuel is not used renew primary energy. Most of energy we use come from fossil fuels, for example, the electricity we use is generated in power stations by burning fossil fuels. The buses we ride use diesel oil. Therefore, we can help reduce the use of fossil fuels by saving energy in our daily lives.

The actions that we can take such as: setting the air-conditioner to a higher temperature, walking instead of using lift, taking a short shower instead of a bath. This reduces the use of the hot water and thus the energy needed to heat the water. Thus, many people can help a lot to reduce our use of fossil fuels to avoid fossil fuel shortage risk occurrence.

For Hong Kong people energy consumption case, how much energy is used when a person travels from Hong Kong to Beijing by airplane? (The distance between Hong Kong and Beijing is about 2000 km). How much energy is used when Hong Kong people take a bus form Tai PO city to Central city? How much energy is used if Hong Kong people drive a car instead? (The driving distance between Tai Po city and Central city is 10Km).

Science explorer, we can visit the England website. Find ways to reduce energy usage from UK people energy using methods. Energy is very important to us. We need energy to walk and carry on any actions. We need energy to grow. We also need energy from food to survive. Without energy, we will die. All machines we use need energy. Without energy the electrical appliances in our homes won't work, the machines in factories will stop.

There are different forms of energy, e.g. light, heat, sound, wind, water, electrical kinetic, chemical and potential energy. Some form energy is primary energy and it can not renew to use, e.g. light, sound, wind, water, fossil fuel etc. Some form energy is secondary energy and it can renew to use in possible, e.g. nuclear, electric charge battery etc. Why does human need to concern how to manufacture secondary energy? Because it is possible that our natural resource will be consumed all, thus we will face primary energy shortage risk. If human can invent any new form of man-made secondary energy to renew to use in order to avoid primary energy shortage to supply to use to use, then human won't only depend on our Earth natural resource energy supply numbers. We can invent any new secondary energy to renew to use again either replaces primary energy or instead of primary energy limit number supply.

What is energy change? For television energy change power case. Firstly, electrical energy changes to television power to be used by television itself, then it changes to light power, next it changes to light power. How to choose fuel form to use? Due to energy can change to different form of powers to supply different form of power advantages to supply to human to use, so it is possible that we can also invent any secondary man made renew used energy to change different form powers to supply us to use, e.g. nuclear energy changes to light or sound or heat form of powers ; electrical charge batteries changes to light or sound or heat form powers to satisfy our daily life needs.

For primary natural resource fuel energy example, different fuel has different feature, e.g. easy to burn, safe to use, gives out a lot of energy, inexpensive, produces little air pollution, easy to transport and store. How can we use in different channels, such as heating food, hot pat, driving vehicles.

For example, although coal is not expensive to cause electricity energy for past transportation tool, e.g. traditional coal energy train or our daily home cooking, but it has negative influence to environment air pollution. Hence, we ought to follow the primary natural resource energy's feature to decide how to apply what aspects of our life needs.

For example, if the country's people hope to reduce pollution when who use any kind of energy, e.g. US , Europe energy markets. The energy entrepreneur ought concentrate on manufacturing the kind of energy which can reduce environment pollution to be the least level to supply the country people to use, e.g. electric charge battery supplies to these countries' drivers to drive their vehicles on the roads, wind energy or water energy to manufacture electricity power supply to reduce air or water pollution ; or if the country people hope to buy the inexpensive energy to use, even the energy's quality and performance is worse, e.g. China, India, Hong Kong markets. The energy entrepreneur ought concentrate on manufacturing the lowest cost and enough supply of natural resource to manufacture the kind of energy to sell cheap price to these countries to use, e.g. China, Africa can accept to use e.g. gas, coal, fuel energy to use to compare developed countries people, e.g. UK, US; or if the countries people who hope to use energy which can easy to transport and store, e.g. light coal. The energy entrepreneur can choose to concentrate on manufacturing much coal to supply to the countries people to use, e.g. China, Arica Thus, to choose to manufacture which kinds of energy supply to the countries market people to use, the energy entrepreneur how decides to manufacture which kind of energy, it depends on which kinds of fuel advantages of the countries people most concerning.

climate change raises secondary energy need

Secondary energy commercial worth

What is energy meaning? It is defined a dynamic quality, it is a fundamental entity of nature that is transferred between parts of a system in the production of physical change within the system, and it is usually regarded as the capacity for doing work, and it is usable power (such as heat or electricity) or the resources for producing such power.

Why does secondary energy own investment worth? Because the different forms of primary natural resource energy will have supply shortage crisis, such as natural resources coal, gas, solar, wind, water, geothermal, biomass(organic material) etc. However, human can attempt to explore any undiscovered Earth or Space resource to manufacture any kinds of secondary energies, e.g. nuclear energy, electric recharge battery energy to supply to electric vehicle or space robots transportation tools to use or satisfy our daily life needs in future one day. So any kind of undiscovered secondary man-made renewed used energy resources have potential commercial worth to any energy entrepreneurs, it is possible that they can replace traditional primary energy to supply to human to use for our different aspects of life needs. In the future, the secondary energy demand will increase, when primary energy supply number has decreased form natural exploration. So, it will cause the effect of any demand of secondary energy product to be raised and prices to be increased in possible.

Due to global population has been growing up, considerably China and India both countries populations have been increasing rapidly. Scientists predict there are more than 1.2 billion people worldwide will lack access to electricity, and more than 2.5 billion still use wood, charcoal to cook and heat in the future when primary energy has no enough number to supply to us to use. Hence, the fact that demand is this much greater than supply to make energy a prime market for further growth.

● Energy investment risks

Although, secondary energy will have much investment worth, but energy like all other investments will carry risks. The internal and external risk factors include such as: policy is always changing to prohibit which do energy trading more easily between the energy exporting and importing countries, the secondary energy manufacturer itself own abilities to invent and to manufacture any kinds of secondary energy, improved technology can quickly make an technology obsolete, geopolitical rifts can happen overnight, the country's energy consumer (user)'s preferable choice to use which either kinds of secondary energy or secondary energy. So, it seems that (man-made) renewed used secondary energy industry can provide above-average returns, but it can also bring high risk commercial investment.

● Ways to solve energy exploration challenge

Traditionally, energy supply companies will apply those methods to operate energy providing businesses. For Shell,. Exxon examples, which had own gas stations, explore and drill for gas on their own. Other companies specialize in a part of the energy market, e.g. leasing oil rigs for example, or operating a pipeline. Energy supplying companies can choose to manufacture any kinds of energy to supply, e.g. trade oil, gas, coal, uranium, electricity etc. Any energy price and supply is demanded on the countries energy users' which kinds of energy most choice need or certain energy commodities to be chose to use popularly. For example, if US most people prefer to use secondary man-made renew used energy more than primary energy. Then, US energy manufacturers ought concentrate on manufacturing much different kinds of secondary man-made renew used energy to prepare to supply to its domestic US market in order to raise secondary energy price to sell in its country. So, the energy manufacturer's energy manufacturing choice, it is depend on which the country's people prefer to use which kinds of energy for their daily life needs.

However, scientists predict secondary energy market will have large market share, due to primary energy will have shortage to explore to supply in our earth and future energy consumers(users) prefer to choose to use more efficiency, less energy consumption, none environment pollution cause, cost effectiveness, renew to use of any kinds of energy. For example, the electricity recharge battery secondary man-made renew used energy is one kind of reducing air pollution power to push any electric battery vehicles to be driven to compare gas energy during drivers are driving their cars on the roads. They can reduce noise and air pollution and drivers can drive safely, who only need to buy one electric recharge battery to recharge in any electric recharge battery stations on streets when the electric recharge battery has no enough power to push their cars and they need to recharge their electric recharge battery drive when they had driven between one to two days. Due to primary energy, e.g. fuel , gas, the kinds of primary energies will have shortage to supply to global drivers to drive their traditional cars. Thus, the electric recharge battery or any undiscovered secondary energy will be future driving market needs. So, man-made renew used secondary energy, e.g. biofuel, hydro-electric, nuclear, will be one kind of efficient, clean, less pollution cause, cost-effective of energy to supply to our global vehicle market, even any other undiscovered new markets. Supposing they are popular to be used for electric vehicle market globally in future one day, then their prices will be decreased and constructed to average car requires up to 1,700 gallons of oil. Also supposing that making average computer requires more than ten times or weight to fossil fuels, every calories of food eaten in the US requires roughly then calories of fossil fuels. Hence, cheap energy will be one successful factor to influence future potential energy consumer (user) individual choice needs. Conversely, ion good economic times, people are more willing to travel, to buy products, and all of which success demand and low process for energy.

● Food production secondary energy need

In the future, secondary energy will be the best choice to food production market. The modern food production system is essentially a success of changing fossil fuels into food. So, raising energy prices are almost higher food costs and even shortage for fossil fuels energy. If one day, one kind of discovered secondary man-made renew used energy can supply to any restaurants or homes to be used to cook at the cheap price, then the profit is very high for this kind of food production energy. Thus, future food production secondary energy consumption market is large and because the primary energy inputs for agriculture are higher than the energy outputs of the food. However, future secondary man-made renew used energy for food production system is only one part of whole energy consumer in food industry. The food production is related to whole food consumption market which includes: household cooking energy market, agriculture or vegetable, rice, fruit etc. foods farming machines energy market, food manufacturing factories market, food machine package market, transportation food delivery market, supermarket or fruit/food sale stores market. They must need any energy inputs to achieve the food production or food transportation or warehouse / stores electricity supply or cooking energy needs. Hence, these food suppliers relate to any whole food factory manufacturers, food retailers, food wholesalers, farmers and home/ restaurant cookers, all of them must need to use energy to carry on their food producing or food cooking or food transportation activities every day in overall food industry. Thus, it seems that undiscovered any second energy demand will be increased, when the primary energy supply number is decreasing. Also, when people can accept to use secondary energy to replace primary energy to be used for any cooking, transporting food, manufacturing food, food retail stores or warehouse food delivery energy need activities. Then, the secondary energy price will be fall down to attract many food energy consumers.

Nowadays, the food industry energy may includes primary nature resource gas energy or electricity energy for house house families or restaurants cooking needs, food delivering lorry drivers driving needs usually. If future second man made renew used energy is invented successful popular to be used, e.g. hydrogen, electric recharged battery energy for electric vehicles or restaurant/home families cooking needs or food factories machine maufacturing energy needs. Then, the seconday energy will have possible to replace primary energy to be food industry energy market.

Wiley, composition services graphics indicated that global primary energy consumption had been increasing 30 billion tons from 1830 year to 510 billion tons in 2010 year as well as global population size had been increasing from 70 billion 1830 yeat to 510 billion in 2010 year. Thus, it seems that global primary energy consumption will be needed largely after 2010 year. If future global nature resource primary energy is explored full number and it had not enough energy number to supply global human to use. Then, it will being many people feel uncomfortable and inconvenient,e.g. Some countries won't have enough energy to supply transportion tools to be driven, some homes and restaurants won't have enough energy to supply to cook to eat or to provide restaurant clients to eat etc. daily activies, due to human's much activities which are needs energy supply. Thus, it seems that global primary energy comsumption will be needed largely after 2010 year.

Wiley, composition services graphics also explianed that why the primary energy consumption demand can be needed to achieve the same level to the global population size increasing in 2010 year. The graph showed these reasons why cause the same level of global population size and global primary energy consumpion demand which may include: The graph showed that after a nation is developed, its per-person energy use hegins to level off. In North Ameruca and Europe, where energy demand has remained flat, or fallen dightly, in each of the past few years. But the 1.3 billion people on those two continents are far outweighted by the 5 billion people in Asia and Africa, e.g. Chinese and Indian. who currently have more energy need to comapre average per man to North America and Europe per man, ensuring that overall energy demand will rise for years to come.

Wiley, composition services graphics also predicted that the growth in primary energy demand. China will have 4,500 million tons in 2035 year. India will have 3,000 million tons in 2035 year. Other developing Asia will have 2,000 million tons in 2035 year. Russia will have 1,500 million tons in 2035, Middle East will have 1,300 million tons in 2035, other rest of world will have 1,000 million tons in 2035. Hence, it implied that China will be the largest primary energy need country in the future.

China will be future the primary potential energy consumer market. The primary energy includes water, coal, wind, fossil oil, gas ,solar, geothermal energy, biomass (organiz material) etc. different natural resource primary energy. Otherwise, US, UK, Europe will be secondary energy potential need market. For example, electrical recharge battery energy will be raised demand to supply to any future new design electrical charge battery vehicles in US, Europe, UK markets.

Due to US, Europe, UK people concern environment protection, so they will invent many electric charge battery vehicles to consume electrical charge battery to replace polluted gas energy to avoid air pollution when the drivers are driving cars on themselve countries' roads. For example, second man-made renew used nuclear energy can be applied to rockets to pusch them to leave our earth to fly to other space far away and consuming nuclear energy will be cost efficient, and nuclear energy saving will be more when nuclear to spend long time to be used in any long time space journey. Hence, nuclear energy and electric charge battery secondary energy will be popular to be applied to vehicles and rockets energy needs in US, Europe, potential marketss, even our daily energy needs in global second energy market.

● Law and policies in engery supply industry

Every energy entrepreneur needs to consider how whose government implement law and policies to prohibit whose energy consumption, energy distribution and energy production behavior in order to protect energy consumers can have fair price energy purchase from the country's energy suppliers between themselves. For US energy law and policy example, the energy independence and security Act of 2007 year. It's major provisions include: Accelerated research of clean energy technologies Act, energy savings in building and industry Act, improved standards for appliances and lighting Act, improved vehical fuel economy Act and increased production of biofuel Act. It aims to prohibit any US energy manufacturing suppliers do any unfair energy trading transaction behavior to its domestic or foreign energy consumers immortally.

● Energy entrepreneur's business strategy

Before you decide to operate either any kinds of secondary energy or primary energy supply business or both kinds of energy supply business. I recommend that you need to consider how to solve these questions before choosing which kind of energy product to manufacture. The questions may include as below:

Who are your energy business's competitors (peers)? How do they compare? How have your energy business company performed cyclically? How to choose to manufacture to sell which kinds of primary or secondary energy product(s), either manufactures only primary energy product(s) or manufactures only secondary energy products or both? Which countries do you plan to sell your energy product?

Illustration by Wilsey, composition services graphiss showed that these natural resources to energy product the world's electricity percentage, such as below:

41% of coal, 5% of oil, 21% of gas, 13% of nuclear, 16% of Hydro, 3% other renewable secondary man-made energy.

Hence, coal will be future the major natural resource to produce electricity. The energy entrepreneur ought attempt to explore any coal resources, when who choose to supply electricity power to consumers for future energy consumption country markets.

Wiley, composition services also predicted that the expectation is that North America coal will supply the expectation is that North America coal will supply Asian demand, Us export terminals have a total capacity of 173 million tommes output. China will drive 16% of the nations total output. China will drive the sea-born demand for coal over for the forcessable future. Chinese energy consumption will grow more than 12 % between 1980 and 2009 years. Though, China heads global demand, India is growing faster in terms of coal imports. Much of the global coal demand will be supplied by Indonesia and Australia. Colombia, Russia, South Africa and Mongolia are also players in global export coal energy resources.

Consequently, I believe that secondary energy will be one kind of new energy product to replace traditional primary energy product for human energy consumption market global needs. Hence, it is right time any energy entrepreneur needs to research how to explore any undiscovered man-made renew used secondary energy products to avoid primary energy shortage crisis occurrence.

Climate raises scientists Understanding efficient distribution
on solar and water energy need

3.1 Understanding solar energy efficient consumption

What is solar energy? Every day, the sun radiates (send out) and enormous amount of energy, called solar energy. It radiates more energy in one day. Then, the world uses in one year. This energy comes from within the sun itself. The sun makes energy in its inner core in a process called nuclear fusion.

Only a small part of the visible radiant energy (light) that the sun emits into space ever reaches the earth enough to supply all our energy needs. Every hour enough solar energy reaches the earch to supply our nation's energy is considered a renewable energy source due to this fact. Today, people use solar energy to heat buildings and water t generate electricity. Solar energy accounts for a very small percentage of U.S. energy less than one percent. Solar energy is used by residences and to generate mostly electricity.

Method to gather solar: A solar collector is one way to capture sunlight and change it into usable clean energy. A closed car on a sunny day is like a solar collector. As sunlight passes through the car's windows, is it absorbed by the seat covers, walls, and floor of the car. The absorbed light changed into heat. The car;s windows let light in, but they don't let all the heat out. A closed car can get very hot!

Which is space heating? It means heating the space inside a building. Today, many homes use solar energy for space heating. A passive solar home is designed to let in as much sunlight as possible. It is like a big solar collector. For example, a passive solar home doesn't depend on mechancial equipment, such as pumps and blowers to heat the house, whereas active solar homes do. It seems that future human can attempt to apply solar energy to use in home conveniently.

How can apply solar energy? Solar energy can be used to heat water. Heating water for bathing, dishwashing and clothes washing is th second largest have energy cost. Installing a solar water heater can reduce home water heating bill be as much as 50 percent. A solar water heater works a lot like solar space heating. For example, installing a solar collector on a house roof where it can capture sunlight. The sunlight heats water in a tank. The hot water is piped to faucets throughout a house, as it would be with an ordinary water heater.

Solar energy can also be used to produce electricity. Two ways to make electricity from solar energy are photovoltaics and solar thermal systems both. However, compared to other ways of making electricity photovoltic systems are expensive. It can cost to 30 cents per kilowats hour to produce efficient from solar cells. Similar to solar cells, solar systms also celled solar power, use solar energy to produce electricity, but in a different way, most solar thermal systems use a solar collector with a mirrored surface to focus sunlight onto a receiver that heats a liquid. However, solar energy has great potential for the future. Solar energy is free, and its supplies are unlimited. It doesn't pollute or otherwise damage the environment. It can't be controlled by any one nation or industry. IF we can improve the technology to harness the sun's power, we may never face energy shortages again.

For active solar home example, passive homes can get 30 to 80 percent of the heat, they need from the sun. They store their heat energy by using think walls and building materials that retain heat well like concrete, stone and even water. For solr water heating another example, solar energy can also be used to heat water for household use. Heating water for bathing and washing is the second largest home energy cost. Installing a solar water heater can cut that cost in half. A solar water heater works a lot like solar space heating. The sunlight heats water and stores it in tank. The hot water is piped to faucets throughout a house, such as it would be with an ordinary water heater. Finally radiant energy to electricity example, solar energy can be used to produce electricity, e.g. solar-powered toys, calculators, many

lighted roadside signs all use solar cells to covert sunlight into electricity.
Next kind of solar electricity manufacturing method is solar power tower. At full peak, estimated electricity generation each year is 155,000 megawatt-hours, enough to power 11,000 homes. This makes the Martin Next generation solar energy center the largest solar thermals power plant in the Eastern United States.

In conclusion, human can earn benefits of solar energy include: Solar electric systems are safe, clean and quiet to operate. Solar systems are highly reliable, solar systems are cost-effective in remote areas and for some residential and commercial applications, solar systems are flexible and can be expanded to meet increasing electrical needs for homes and businesses, solar systems can provide independence from the grid on backing during outages, the fuel is renewable and free and domestically produced, harnessing solar energy spurs economic development, using solar energy to generate electricity produces no greenhouse gases. Hence, future solar energy will be a kind of renewable and reused and recycled natural resource energy to be provided to human to use.

3.2 Understanding water energy efficiency
The efforts to improve water and efficiency from both the supply and the demand sides would allow countries to reduce resource scarcity and maximize water energy benefits. However, water efficiency is a concept, it means " doing more and better with less by obtaining more value with the available resources by reducing the resource consumption and reducing the pollution and environmental impact of wate use for the stage of the value chain and of water service provision."
Improving water efficiency means increasing water productivity, reducing the intensity of water use for, and pollution from socio-economic activities through maximizing. The value of the uses of water, improving the allocation of water greater socio-economic value per drop of water in order to achieve aim to ensure environmental flows, and improving technical efficiency of water services and the management efficiency of their provision over the complete life cycles.
How to enable water and energy efficiency? Water thirsty energy demonstrates the importance of combined energy and water management approaches through demand-based work in several countries. In order to ensure water energy users to earn water energy efficient benefits.
How to make the right choice among water resource efficient technologies?

These include recycling and reuse of water, low water using appliances, efficient irrigation systems, decentralized sewerage systems, information and communication technologies, rainwater caterments and reclamation of nutrients and creating new opportunities to water renewable energy potential and the need of innovatin and development and serves to solve energy shortage from water renewable and reused resource energy invention.

Water energy efficient production method includes, it will allow differentiating between water withdrawal, water consumption and net water consumption and calculating different kinds of interactions between the activity and its water environment. With an annual investment of US$198 billion on average over the next forty years, water use can be made more efficient, enabling increased agricultural, biofuels, and industrial production (UNEP, 2011).

Investing US$170 billion annuallly in energy efficiency worldwide could produce energy savings of up to US$900 billion per year (SE4ALL, 2012) and each additional US$1 spent on energy efficiency in electrical equipment, appliances and buildings avoids more than US$2 on average in energy supply investments (IEA, 2012).

How can water energy distribution solution? The facilitate greater operational efficiency including energy-efficient water supply operation systems and water distribution control systems that help in ways that include reducing electricity costs as well as the load on the environment. For one example to water distribution solution for more efficient operation of water supply and individual technologies. The water distributin system will consist first stage is component technology to (linear programming and modeling). Second stage is solution: water supply, it is operation and planning techniques that works with electronic power demand response. The final stage is water source, water will be intaked to aqueduct them to deliver water treatment plant. Next step, the water treatment plant water will be delivered to main water pipe. Final stage, water will be delivered to water distribution network from water distribution network to this whole water distribution process. It depends on the time of day. Incentive schemes, such as load control programs request users to reduce their power use at times when the supply of electric power is constrained and pay them for doing so in the form of a bonus from water power station suppliers. So, nowadays, some countries' water power station supplies have developed a water supply operation technique that reduces electricity costs by earning these incentives.

What is water supply operation technique? The water supply operation technique consists of operation mode that seeks to smooth electric power use in ways that cut the basic tariff by smoothing demand across the course of day and a demand response operation mood that earns incentives by reducing demand in response to requests. Water supply surplus uses a large number of distribution reservoirs to buffer the gap between demand for water and the supply from the water treatment plants.

Furthermore, falling demand in recent years means there are a significant number of distribution reservoirs with excess capacity. This means that peaks in electricity demand can be shifted or cut by taking advantage of this unused water storage capacity to shift the timing of conveying pump operation. Minimising electric power consumption as far as possible during demand peaks or during time periods specific in demand response requires. But, it also requires risk management to ensure that the water levels in distribution reservoirs don't full below their lower limits. Consequently, water supply will be another kind of reused energy resource to provide to human to use.

What is future household energy consumption trend?

In general, household energy consumption includes , i.e. for lighting, cooking, heating etc. The household sector is responsible for about 15 to 25 percent of primary energy use for a higher share in many developing countries. Average per capita household energy use in developed countries is about nine time higher than in developing countries, even though in developing countries a large share of household energy is provided by non-commercial fuels are historical trends in per capita household energy consumption by these kinds of energy, i.e. fuel, coal, petroleum, natural gas and electicity etc. energy.

Some scientists indicate Asia and South America have consequently lower energy efficiency. However, the major factors contributing to countries which lower and higher energy efficiency differences include, such as levels of urbanizatin, economic development and living standards. Other factors are country or region specific, such as climate or cultural practices. However, energy efficiency depends both in the types of fuel used and on the characteristics of particular appliances.

Consequently, future trend of energy will be renewable, reused, cheap more efficient and productive secondary energy for human to use.

Reference

Sustainable energy for ALL (SE4ALL) initiative, United Nations secretary.
http://www.sustainableenergyforall.org

Towards a green economy pathways to sustainable development and poverty eradication. Unites Nations Environment programe (UNEP), 2011
http://www.unep.org/greeneconomy

World energy outlook, executive summary, p.7 IEA , 2012

FOUR

HOW CLIMATE INFLUENCES MIGRANTS DESIRES

Impact of population growth and population ethics on climate change mitigation

Future population growth migration number is uncertain, due to climate change factor influence. Higher mitigation growth entails more emissions and means either more people will choose to mitigate other better climate countries to live or the better climate countries will have more people to immigrate to live, due to any sudden climate change environment related impacts.

However, some climate scientists feel how future population is related importantly determines mitigation decisions. They indicated that some bad climate countries' people make any mitigation decision choice, it responds to the fact that a larger population means climate change hurts more people. For example, in 2025 year assuming United Nations has high rather than low population scenario entails an increase in the social cost of carbon dioxide (SCC) of 85% under total utilitarianism (TU), vs 5% under average utilitarianism (AU). The difference is the (SCC) between the two population scenarios under (TU) is comparable to commonly debated decisions regarding time discounting. Additionally, they estimate the avoided mitigation costs implied by reductions in population growth, finding that large neat term savings US $6billions amount annually occur under (TU). Hence, it seems that climate changing is one important factor to bring any bad climate change countries which need to pay large disaster expenditure to recover their economy after any sudden serious climate change impacts.

4.1

How climate change impacts on developing countries

In fact, climate change will increase global temperature change rainfall patterns and will result in more frequent and severe floods and drought. Depending on future emission of greenhouse gases, global temperatures are likely to rise between 2 degree and 4 degree within the next century. The main impacts of climate change will however not be felt through higher temperatures, but through a change in the hydrological cycle. Rainfall is likely to increase around the poles and the tropics when in the sub-tropics average precipitation is likely to decrease. Not only the average annual or seasonal rainfall will change, there also be an increase in the number of extreme events resulting in most frequent and severe floods and droughts.

How does climate change influence to development countries? Climate change will influence any development countries on these several aspects. They include as below:

On trade influence hand, reducing emission levels from the developing world is extremely important. If current developments are continuing, for example, emissions from China and India both countries will save be much higher than the total emission form all Europe countries. Currently, the Europe is stimulating mitigation and transfer of clean technologies through the clean development mechanism (CDM). Although, it is still unclear what the mitigation potential of the (CDM) is, especially in India the investment is (CDM) projects is significant. However, the Europe should take a much wider approach. In developing countries a lot can be done in terms of increasing energy efficiency, land use change and agriculture. It is also important that developing countries are stimulated to choose a sustainable, low emission developed pathway. Choices for more sustainable, low emission technologies should be made early in the process. It seems that climate changing will encourage many countries will choose to do more environment protection related trading, e.g. researching how to invent environment protection new products to reduce our earth pollution between European and any developing countries, such as China and India etc.

On focus mitigation efforts in least developed countries on land use change, agriculture development aspect, in the least developed countries mitigation efforts should not focus on the energy or transport sector, but on agriculture and forestry. Agriculture is responsible for a relatively large percentage of the emissions in many developing countries, e.g. Africa, China, Malaysia, Hong Kong, Japan etc. In this sector there are many win options both reducing poverty and reducing greenhouse gas emissions. For example, improved water and nutrient management can sharply increase production efficiency and reduces at least the amount of emission per kg food produced. Agro-forestry reduces greenhouse gas emission through increased carbon storage and reduces poverty through diversifying the incomes of local communities.

However, in most developing countries, the main limitation in coping with the impacts of climate change is a lack of capacity. Besides a lack of capacity, in many developing countries, there is also a significant lack of data and knowledge on climate change impacts. Developing countries should be stimulated to improve data gathering and make existing data more easily available.However, no migration effort will stop the need for adaptation. Especially, the least developed countries, who have contributed little to the problem will suffer the most.

On business strategies for climate change aspect, nowadays, the valuation for clean-technology companies, have increased considerable and the corporate carbon footprint has become an important topic to be discussed how to solve among senior managers? How can firms profit from what they do to address climate change? Thus, a low-carbon economy is already especially in energy, transport and heavy industry.

If current climate science holds true and there is considerable uncertainty in the estimates, global greenhouse gas emissions should ideally decrease from today's levels by 90 percent as of 2050 year in order to certain global warming below two degrees centigrade. Hence, it seems global warmth challenge brings further any new energy potential development businesses. Due to environment scientists encourage us to be realized the necessary increase in carbon productivity and new low-carbon technologies that are necessary dramatically reduces energy consumption and direct greenhouse gas emissions will have to be developed and then implemented widely to avoid future serious global environment warmth caused climate changes and pollution challenges occurrence.

4.2

Does health reason influence developing countries people to choose migration by climate change impact?

Climate change is caused substantial increases in population movement. It has considered the likely causal influences much movement and the risks to national and international security. But, there has been little research on the consequences of climate-related migration and the health of people who move. May health impacts of climate change play important role in population movement?

However, climate change-related migration is likely to result in adverse health outcomes, particularly in situations of forced migration. In fact, climate change is widely projected to cause substantial increases in the scale of human population movement. Forecasts of the number of people who will move by around midcentury in response to the effects of climate change vary from tens of millions to 250 million people (United Nations High Commissions For Refugees (UNHCR, 2009).

Many scientists believe migration reason is common that the countries' people are fear of diseases and climate change environmental disasters to be caused in their countries, especially developing countries by climate change negative influences. Specially, populations in low-income countries whose health is most at risk from climate changes and where. There are often high pre-existing levels of health problems are used to coping with adverse health outcomes without causing to migration. So, it is likely that population movement that is driven substantially by health risks will occur only where those risks are sufficiently serious and widespread. For example, Africa the country's climate change will bring the risk of infectious disease (e.g. cholera , measles, malaria, meningitis) to Africa. In fact, Africa has adequate health care systems, low immunization coverage, lack of clean water and poor sanitation (Zarocostas, 2011).

Thus, it seems that climate change will bring health risk challenge to the country to influence people to choose to migrate other countries. Although, the range and extent of health risks with future climate related population movements can't be clearly forever, but the evidence of health outcomes of movement of people indicates that health risks will predominate over health benefits. This often is an issue of considerable geopolitical, ethical and economic importance. Consequently, it has close cause and effect relationship between climate change and health risk to cause people to choose migration.

What is developing countries people's acceptable climate change adaptive level

Nowadays, climate change influences those developing countries, such as Africa, China, India, Hong Kong etc. which people's standard of life to be worse seriously. Moreover, such as other Asia, Latin America and small country regions which are facing climate change negative influence seriously. How can these countries' people who can adapt climate change influence to live in themselves countries? Climate change causes these challenges to above these countries, such as facing shortage of clean natural water and food and greater risks to health and life.

Some scientists predicted under a business as usual scenario, greenhouse gas emissions could rise by 25 pre cent to 90 per cent by 2030 year relative to 2000 year and the Earth could warm by 3 degree this century. Even with a temperature rise of 1.25 degree, the predict serious effects including reduced crop yields in topical areas leading to increased risk of hunger, spread of climate sensitive diseases, such as climate sensitive diseases, such as malaria, and an increased risk of extinction of 20 to 30 per cent. Hence, developing countries need international assistance, transfer of technology and capacity building are also needed to reduce the risk of disasters and raise the resilience of communities to increasing extreme events, such as droughts, floods, and tropical cyclones.

However, developing countries have very different individual circumstances and the specific impacts of climate change on a country depend on the climate it experiences as well as its geographical, social, cultural, economic and political situations. The main influence sectors of climate change include: agriculture, water resources, human health, terrestrial ecosystems and biodiversity and coastal zones, even the issue concerns that many developing countries' human migration to other better climate countries to live to cause labor supply shortage challenge in developing countries.

Adaption is a process through when societies make themselves better able to cope with an uncertain future. Adapting to climate change entails taking the right measures to reduce the negative effects of climate change (or exploit the positive ones) by making the appropriate adjustments and changes. There are many options and opportunities to adapt. These range from technologies options, such as increases sea defenses or flood proof houses on stilts to behavior change at the individual level, such as reducing welfare use in times of drought and using insecticide-sprayed mosquito nets. Other strategies include early warming systems for extreme events, better water management, improved risk management, various insurance options, and biodiversity conservation.

Because of the speed at which change is happening, due to global temperature rise. So, adaption plans are needed to implement to developing countries. However, assessing the impacts to climate change and subsequently working and adaptions needs requires good quality information. They include climate data, such as temperature rainfalls and the frequency of extreme events, and non-climate data, such as the current situation on the ground for different sectors including water resources, agriculture and food security, human health, terrestrial ecosystems and bio-diversity, and coastal zones.

For countries to understand their coal climate better and thus be able to predict local climate change, they must have adequate operational national systematic observing networks, and access to the data available from other global and regional networks, systematic observations of the climate system are usually carried out by national meteorological centers and other specialized centers.

They take observations at standard present times and places and monitor atmosphere, ocean and terrestrial systems. The major climate variables measured include temperature, rainfall, sea surface temperature, sea level rise, wind speeds tropical cyclones (including hurricanes and typhoons), snow and ice over. For example, monitoring trends of sea surface temperature add sea level are essential in order to assess their impacts on the increases intensity of tropical cyclones and storm surge; monitoring events relating to the phenomenon (ENSO) is important in helping determining its effects on reducing or increasing precipitation in different regions leading to both floods and drought.

For China example, it is one considerable climate change country, it is monitoring atmospheric composition, energy balance, water and carbon cycles, ecosystems and land use, ice and snow and regularly submits real time observation data of China GCOS stations and historical data records from national stations to the world fata center for meteorology. The country has an operational system of short term climatic monitoring, prediction and assessment, established in the Beijing China city climate center and it has some regional cooperative climate programs with other Asian developing countries, such as Islamic Republic of Iran, Nepal etc.

Thus, we can image that China, India, Africa have many people to live and their population growth speed is fast every year. If future one day climate change has reached the serious and non control level to these both countries to let them feel difficult to adapt to live in their countries. Then, the effect will possible be many Chinese and India and Africa people choose to migrate to other better climate countries to live at the same time. It will bring these countries challenge , such as shortage of young people labor supply when their countries' many young people choose to leave their home countries to migrate to other better climate countries to live as well as the better climate countries will have many worse climate countries' young people to immigrate to their countries to compete to their domestic young people to seek jobs in their labor market at the same time suddenly. However, if their local jobs are not enough to supple to both domestic and foreign young people to do in the long time suddenly.

It will cause unemployment challenge to the better climate countries, even it will bring young theft, fighting social behavioral crime and their crime number will increase suddenly when many young people have no jobs to work and no effort money to live in better climate countries. Even, worse climate developing countries' people will be unhealthy to bring any illnesses to the better climate countries to let the people feel difficult to live in their countries. Thus, we can't neglect that bad climate changing challenge will bring the developing countries young people to feel difficult adaption to live issue. Thus, if developed countries expect to avoid shortage of jobs to supply, unemployment, social crime etc. challenges, due to the sudden migration/ immigration number increases from the bad climate change developing countries. It is the best time to seek any solvable methods to avoid the sudden bad climate change occurrence.

The cause and effect relationship between climate change and environment migration

The choice of migration reasons can include that seeking better job chance, better job environment, better salary, better standard of life, better education, less crimes, feeling more safety etc. different psychological reasons. However, whether climate changing will be one factor to cause migration. This is one psychological life adaption issue. Some people may accept to adapt to live worse life when their countries are encountering any natural environment or economic negative or climate negative change or social negative impact suddenly. Otherwise, some people may not accept to adapt to live worse life when they countries are encountering any worse influences suddenly, such as sudden worse climate change. Thus, to research that whether it has relationship to influence migration choice between climate change and migration. We need to know whether what the general acceptable level to adapt climate change to human is.

It means that if the climate change has exceeded the countries' general people's acceptable level to adapt to live in their countries. Then, it is possible that it will cause many people do not feel more adaptive to live in their countries forever, due to serious sudden climate change disaster occurrence.

What is the general acceptable level to live to their countries to adaptive climate change? However, before they choose to migrate, they will mind these questions usually. How can they migrate? Once they leave, who will guard their land? How will they support their family in the city?

Environment problems are both sudden and gradual have always causal different formed of displacement around the world, but recent studied have emphasized that more people are likely to migrate in the future, owing to climate change (Stern, N. 2007).

In fact, climate change will bring serious challenge to any countries, such as natural resources shortage, lacking more productive livelihoods supply. Then, it views this question: If migration have no adaptive potential, then what can be done (or is being done) to facilitate communities to migrate? Analyzing

who migrants, how, why and where they go can provide useful insights for development planners aiming to support poor families. It seems that every family member's adaptive to live factor will influence the whole family who decides to choose to migrate or stay in their country when climate change disaster sudden occurs.

However, environmental migration is typically internal and short term, the potential for conflict is that unstable urban and rural demographics are related to higher risks of civil war and low level conflicts to environment migration during periods of environmental stress are common. Also, I believe that the impact of climate change can be divided into two distinct drivers of migration:

Climate processes driver , such as sea-level rise, shortage of agricultural land, desertification and growing water scarcity and climate events , such as flooding, storms. But, non-climate drivers, such as government policy, population growth and community level resilience to natural disaster are also important. All contribute to the degree of people's adaptive level.

The climate change problem is one of time (the speed of change) and scale (the number of people it will affect). Although, temporary migration is as an adaptive response to climate stress is already apparent in many areas. But the ability to migrate is a function of mobility and resources (both financial and social). IN other words, the people most to climate change are not necessary the one's most likely to migrate among of different migration factors.

In fact, predicting future flows of climate migrants is complex. Professor Myers' estimate of 200 million climate migrants by 2050 year has become the accepted figure-cities in respected publications from the IPCC to the Stern Review on the economics of climate change (Stern, N., Ed. 2006).Hence, it seems that there will have many different factors to cause climate migrant number rising in the future.

Consequently, migration and resettlement may be the most threatening short-term effects of climate change on human settlements. People may decide to migrate in any of the following cases. They includes: loss of housing (because of river, or sea flooding or mudslides), loss of living resources (like water, energy and food supply or employment affected by climate changes); loss of social and cultural resources (loss of cultural properties, neighborhood or community networks).

The three main climate change impacts to influence people to live may include that sea level rise: rising average sea level, sale water intrusion in aquifers, water availability (increase/decrease), extreme weather event: drought, heat waves, violent storms, floods. Thus, if any one of these environment change factors impacts to influence general people's life adaptive level to live anywhere in their any geographic location of their countries. Then, it is possible to influence them to choose to be environmental migrants. It means persons or group of persons who, for compelling reasons of sudden or progressive changes in the environment that adversely affect their lives or living conditions are obliged to leave their habitual homes, or choose to do so, either temporarily or permanently and who move either within their country or abroad. Thus, climate change can let them to feel that it is one unsafe natural disaster and it only brings negative effect to them when they still choose to live in their home town. It refers to situations where people are displaced across boarders in the context of sudden or slow onset disasters or in the context of the adverse effects of climate change.

In forces to non-forces mobility psychological view point, environmental refugee will have these three stages to decide migration: First stage is , refugee –like situation stage, it is very low level control over the whole process , vulnerability. Second stage is, environmentally driven displacement stage, it is compelled, but voluntary, more control over timing and direction and less vulnerability than refugees, but less control and more vulnerability than migrants. Final stage is migrant like situations stage, it is greater control over the process and less vulnerability , even if people are moving in response to deteriorating conditions (Hugo, G. 1996).

Consequently, climate change will be one main important factor to cause any country people who choose to do environmental migrants decision to compare other factors. IT seems, that climate change factor and environment migrant which have close relationship to cause any country people who choose to migrate more than social , economy , less crime, education, cultural , job change, standard of life etc. different external non-natural environment factors.

Reference

Hugo, G. (199). Environmental concerns and
International migration. International migration
Review., 30. Pp. 105-131.

Mendelsohn , R., (2013) " Climate Change And Economic Growth Commission On Growth And Development" working paper no 60.
Stern, N., (ed.) The economics of climate change: The Stern Review, Cambridge University Press,
Cambridge, 2006, p.3.

Stern, N. (2007). The Economics Of Climate Change: The Stern Review, Cambridge UK:
University Press.

UNHCR/WFP (United Nations High Commission For Refugees) World Food Program, 2009. Acute Malnutrition in protected refugee situation: A global strategy Geneva: UNHCR/WFP.

Zarocostas , J. 2011. Famine and disease threaten millions in drought hit horn of Africa. BMJ 343: doi: 10,1136/bmj.d4a4a <online 21 July 2011>.

The relationship between climate and
migrant desire
How climate change influences migrant right change
How and why climate change influence migrant right change ? When

migrant right change, how it influence migrant immigrating desire ? The interlinkages between climate change and human rights are deep and complex, with climate change impacting a wide range of internationally protected human rights; such as rights to health and even life and rights to food, water, shelter and property. In this paper, I am going to discuss the effect of climate change on protected human rights relating to migration, focusing primarily on the relationship between international refugee law and climate change.

There remains uncertainty on how severe global warming will be and its precise impacts on society, but there is a 97 per cent consensus among experts that a rapid build-up of greenhouse gas is due to human activities.The Earth's climate is gradually changing due to the continuous concentration of anthropogenic greenhouse gas (GHG) emissions into the atmosphere. The Earth's surface temperature is getting warmer at a disturbing rate, and has become significantly warmer in the last 150 years after 10,000 years of relative stability.[3] Most climate change projections are based on a two-degree Celsius increase in global mean temperature from the temperature in 1850, which has now been agreed by most States as the threshold for 'dangerous' climate change.

The consequences of climate change are more obvious now due to the increased prevalence of rising sea levels, extreme weather conditions, drought and desertification, and these consequences will have significant effects on the ecosystem, specifically on food security, migration, and health. The political, economic, and social capacity of a country, which includes its infrastructure, economic stability, and ability to help its population when in need, will affect individual's ability to cope with the impacts of climate change, and therefore the impacts will be felt differently in different communities. In the 1980s and 1990s, climate change was primarily viewed as an environmental and scientific issue, but in 1990 the potential impacts of climate change on human migration were identified by the Intergovernmental Panel on Climate Change (IPCC). The IPCC stated that millions of people would likely be uprooted by shoreline erosion, coastal flooding, and agricultural disturbances (such as salination of crops),and that climate change might require consideration of 'migration and resettlement outside of national boundaries.

However, the relationship between climate change and forced migration has emerged as one of the most studied, but contested, fields of inquiry, and the lack of agreement on the links between climate change and forced migration explains why the call for the recognition of so-called 'climate change refugees' has been unsuccessful. Legally, there is no such thing as a 'climate change refugee,' and this point will be expanded upon later in this paper, but there is, however, evidence that people are moving in response to the effects of climate change. Cross-border displacement resulting from natural disasters and the effects of climate change has therefore been identified as a normative gap in the international legal protection regime.Determining how exactly climate change affects people's decisions to move is crucial in determining how appropriate the call for the inclusion of people displaced by gradual or sudden environmental impacts within the refugee protection framework.

As discussed above, there is an ongoing debate and scepticism as to the direct link between climate change and displacement, but there is now mounting evidence which supports the plight of so-called 'climate change refugees' and demands attention from the international legal community. The term 'climate change refugee' is often used to describe those who will be forced to leave their homes because of climate change impacts. In this section, I will focus on the extent to which international refugee law may apply, and discuss why, by and large, it is an inappropriate framework for responding to the needs of the displaced.

The first official use of the term 'climate change refugee' was by Essam El-Hinnawi in a United Nations Environment Programme (UNEP) report, where he described people who are forced to leave their places of residence because of human or naturally induced environmental issues as 'environmental refugees'. El-Hinnawi was not trying to make a legal argument for the extension of refugee law to cover those displaced for environmental reasons, but instead was using the term to highlight the potentially devastating effects of unchecked development and pollution. Since then the term has been used in almost any discussion involving the impacts of climate change and forced migration. While those displaced internally (within their own countries) can be protected using the United Nations Guiding Principles on Internal Displacement mechanism, or even by the national law of their own countries, those displaced by environmental impacts and who are crossing or wish to cross their countries' borders currently have no legal basis for this type of movement in international law.

The relationship between climate change, natural disasters, and migration

What is the positive or negative impacts when climate change causes disasters and then bring migration number increases or decreases? The relationship between climatic shocks, natural disasters, and migration has received increasing attention in recent years and is quite controversial. One view suggests that climate change and its associated natural disasters increase migration. An alternative view suggests that climate change may only have marginal effects on migration. Knowing whether climate change and natural disasters lead to more migration is crucial to better understand the different channels of transmission between climatic shocks and migration and to formulate evidence-based policy recommendations for the efficient management of the consequences of disasters.

What are the positive and negative impacts when climate change causes natural disasters and migration attributes? I shall indicate as below:

On migration benefit aspect, it may include these such as: migration can help people cope with the adverse effects of climatic shocks by providing them with new opportunities and resources. Remittances from overseas migrants increase after disasters in their home countries and play an important role in mitigating the adverse effects of climatic shocks and natural disasters. Climatic factors, such as natural disasters or rainfall and temperature variations, may increase international migration through their effect on internal migration. Agricultural productivity represents one of the pathways that can explain the relationship between climatic shocks and migration.

However, climate change may also bring these disadvantages on migration benefit aspect, they may include such as: Public intervention both before and after disasters helps build resilience and can explain why migration responses differ according to different shocks. The migration response to disasters depends on the nature of the shock (slow vs rapid onset events), its severity, and the vulnerability of the affected people.Due to liquidity constraints, poor people might not be able to migrate in the aftermath of climatic shocks. Also, in developing countries, international migration due to disasters may be driven by highly educated people, which may foster brain drain in a vulnerable context.

Climate Change and the Migrant Crisis

What is climate change and migrant crisis ? It may include as below:

For India example, when climate change , it can influence India migrant decision. India has the first airport which is solely functioning on solar energy. The world can learn from India or China. The West has to stop dumping subsidized agar products into third world destroying local agar industry and pushing people into poverty. Western fisheries are just taking all fish from coasts of Africa. If these policies continue, europeans dont complain people coming to your countries. For afria example, Africa has tripled their population from 400 million to over 1.2 billion people in the past 40 years. Overpopulation, not climate change is their root problem. Africa now has 1 and quarter billion Africans living in some of the world's wort market places. This new lie (scheme) is a dreamed up scheme to import as many as they can into the first world market places, Europe, u.s., Australia, place them on welfare, make the tax payers foot the bill for all the goods and services they can consume to maximize annualized corporate profits making, and to turn them into citizens and have the tax payers pay to educate them so hopefully they will in the future expand taxes uptake for the government's. All paid for by the tax payers. you get to be absorbed genetically. So, it seems that climate change will bring more negative impact to migrants , when the country can attract many migrants choose to emigrate to the county to live, due to climate change infuences.

● Vulnerable countries number will increase when climate change become worse to influence human live as well as human needs to learn new skills to adapt difficult lives

The relationship between migration and the environment is not new. From the mid-19th century Great Irish Famine to the early 20th century Dust Bowl, we have many examples in history of people choosing or being forced to migrate because of changes in their physical environments. What is new now is that the world is grappling with the devastating impacts of climate change. With greater awareness came increased political recognition and there is now a widespread consensus on the need to address the adverse impacts of climate change on the migration of people now and in the future.

Climate migration is a reality in all parts of the world, however, the situation in what is known as "vulnerable countries" represents a particular challenge. Vulnerable countries are Least Developed Countries (LDCs), Landlocked Developing Countries (LLDCs) and Small Island Developing States (SIDS). In 2016, the 15 countries with the highest vulnerability to natural hazards were LDCs, LLDCs and SIDS. These countries are disproportionately affected by the negative impacts of climate change and are often least able to cope due to their structural constraints and geographical disadvantages. At the same time, they contribute the least to climate change. These countries are among the strongest advocates for more robust action on climate migration as they face very real challenges that affect all aspects of the daily lives of their populations.

Climate migration challenges take multiple forms in these vulnerable countries. In LDCs, the poorest and most vulnerable segment of the international community, climate change pressures can intersect with numerous development-related challenges as well as security issues. The combination of those factors often leads people to migrate in search of better or safer lives. For example, the Lake Chad Basin is currently experiencing grave environmental degradation, in a context where populations face the violence linked to the presence of groups such as Boko Haram. Migration patterns in that region have been reshaped due to these factors. Some LDCs such as Ethiopia and Bangladesh are sometimes saddled with the "double stress" of having to deal with internal climate migration, while also hosting large numbers of refugees from neighboring countries. LLDCs often have scarce water resources, further depleted by the impacts of climate change. This can create pressure on populations to migrate for better access to water. For example, nomadic pastoralists are often pushed to alter their traditional routes and travel further and for longer periods in search of water and land resources. Climate change is also affecting livelihoods, such as in Mongolia where extremely cold winters called dzud deplete nomadic livestock and destroy agriculture opportunities, pushing rural populations to migrate to urban centers.

SIDS are recognized as a special case for sustainable development as they face greater risk of marginalization due to their small size and remoteness. They also have fragile natural environments, and natural disasters such as storms and cyclones have a devastating impact on the population. The adverse impacts of climate change have contributed to the migration of thousands of people in SIDS in the last decade alone. One specific type of migration in this context is the planned relocation of people, where entire communities need to be moved, generally further inland, to escape climate change impacts such as coastal erosion. In Fiji, following Tropical Cyclone Winston in 2016, more than 60 villages were relocated to reduce people's exposure and vulnerability to further risks.

The current situation is clearly preoccupying and addressing the negative impacts of climate change on the migration of people in vulnerable countries should represent a priority now and for the future. We are moving towards a high level week of crucial political dialogues at the United Nations General Assembly in September 2019. In particular, the United Nations

Climate Action Summit is a key opportunity to highlight the challenges of most vulnerable countries and put forward commitments and solutions to address climate migration issues.

On conclusion, riority should be given to mitigate the impacts of climate change and promote climate change adaptation in places where populations are at risk of forced migration. However, it is also clear that in some places, it will not be possible for populations to remain in situ and it is of utmost importance to think about how legal migration options can be offered to those migrants. It is also important to factor in the positive role that migrants can play in the fight against climate change, such as by facilitating remittances and transfer of skills and knowledge towards climate action. So, climate change influences human needs to change skills to adapt difficult lives.

FIVE

CLIMATE CHANGE HOW INFLUENCES HUMAN WORKING BEHAVIORAL CHANGES

Artificial intelligence bank service working environment
Focus on outcomes not technology.Artificial Intelligence: Waiting to be unleashed? The Insider Column - When Digital Transformation misses. Are you meeting the demands of the new digital consumer? Will your legacy mindset compromise your digital competitiveness? Can artificial intelligence create online remote office new business service market in global ?
The Future of Artificial Intelligence In The Workplace:
Is AI going to displace workers or come as a benefit to them?
Is AI going to displace workers or come as a benefit to them? Getty
Smart technologies aren't just changing our homes; they're edging their way into their numerous industries and are disrupting the workplace. Artificial Intelligence (AI) has the potential to improve productivity, efficiency and accuracy across an organization – but is this entirely beneficial? Many fear that the rise of AI will lead to machines and robots replacing human workers and view this progression in technology as threat rather than a tool to better ourselves.
With AI continuing to be a prominent online office service business to replace human actual office working environment, businesses need to

realize that self-learning and black-box capabilities are not the panacea. Many organisations are already beginning to see the incredible capabilities of AI, using these advantages to enhance human intelligence and gain real value from their data. As there is increasing evidence demonstrating the benefits of intelligent systems, more decision-makers in the boardroom are gaining a better understanding of what AI can really offer. Research conducted by EY explains "organizations enabling AI at the enterprise level are increasing operational efficiency, making faster, more informed decisions and innovating new products and services." Can articial intelligent technology create remote office working environment to replace our traditional actual office work environment ? Can we do not need to go to office to work , when any office staffs ,e.g. managers, clerk, etc. they can apply artificial intelligent technology and online technology to work at home, such as remote office working environment ?

The first companies employing AI systems across the board will gain competitive advantage, reduce cost of operations and remove head counts. Whilst this may be a positive from a business perspective, it is obvious why this a worry for those working in roles at risk of displacement. The introduction of these technologies will likely trigger an issue with unions and job security due to the substantial operational changes. Although AI will affect every sector in some way, not every job is at equal risk. PwC predicts a relatively low displacement of jobs (around 3%) in the first wave of automation, but this could dramatically increase up to 30% by the mid-2030's. Occupations within the transport industry could potentially be at much greater risk, whereas jobs requiring social, emotional and literary abilities are at the lowest risk of displacement.

A positive future with artificial intelligence to bring remote online office working environment chance:

Many businesses and individuals are optimistic that this AI-driven shift in the workplace will result in more jobs being created than lost. As we develop innovative technologies, AI will have a positive impact on our economy by creating jobs that require the skill set to implement new systems. 80% of respondents in the EY survey said it was the lack of these skills that was the biggest challenge when employing AI programs.

It is likely that artificial intelligence will soon replace jobs involving repetitive or basic problem-solving tasks, and even go beyond current human capability. AI systems will be making decisions instead of humans in industrial settings, customer service roles and within financial institutions.

Automated decisioning will be responsible for tasks such as approving loans, deciding whether a customer should be onboarded or identifying corruption and financial crime.

Organisations will benefit from an increase in productivity as a result of greater automation, meaning more revenue will generated. This thus provides additional money to spend on supporting jobs in the services sector.Due to the vast array of jobs that could be impacted by AI, it is fundamental to address the potential pitfalls of these technologies. Business need to overcome the trust and bias issues surrounding AI by achieving an effective and successful implementation that makes it possible for everyone to benefit.

Governments must ensure that gains from AI are shared widely across society to prevent social inequality between those affected and unaffected by these developments. For example, this could be through increased investment into training. With the additional cost-savings from implementing AI systems, employers should also focus on upskilling their current employees.

To properly leverage the power of AI, we need to address the issue at an educational level, as well as in business. Education systems needs to focus on training students in roles directly associated to working with AI, including programmers and data analysts. This requires more emphasis to be put on STEM subjects (science, technology, engineering and mathematics). Also, subjects centered around building creative, social and emotional skills should be encouraged. Whilst artificial intelligence will be more productive than human workers for repetitive tasks, humans will always outperform machines in jobs requiring relationship-building and imagination. Hence, artificial intelligence will change our world both inside and outside the workplace. Instead of focusing on the fear surrounding automation, businesses need to embrace these new technologies to ensure they implement the most effective AI systems to enhance and compliment human intelligence.

Artificial Intelligence (AI) in Banking working environment
Artificial Intelligence (AI) is a fast-evolving technology, gaining popularity all around the world. Several industries have already adopted AI for various applications, getting better and smarter day by day. In the past few years, the banking sector has also become one of the leading adopters of Artificial Intelligence. Most banks and financial institutions are implementing AI to

add more efficiency to their back-office and lessen security risks.

As per Statista, the AI market in the United States is forecasted to reach 7.35 billion U.S. dollars in 2018. Some major applications of AI include classification, image recognition, object identification, and automated geophysical feature detection. Speaking of banking and financial institutions, JPMorgan Chase, Wells Fargo, Bank of America, CitiBank, and other leading U.S. banks have already implemented AI in their systems, helping consumers manage their daily banking needs more efficiently.

AI technology can bring better Customer Support in bank service environment

Several pieces of evidence advocate that the customers willingly prefer self-service options which allow them to chat with a virtual assistant as if it were a live customer representative. Most leading banks have already added virtual assistants to their instant website chatbots, voice response systems, and mobile applications. Artificial Intelligence considers each interaction as a teachable moment, so the chatbots (virtual assistants) keeps getting better while understanding customers. With AI, virtual assistants can deliver better customer support. It also allows sentiment analysis, so the virtual assistant can determine when individuals are getting frustrated and instantly transfer them to a live agent.

Enhanced Banking Services

AI streamlines the banking process while giving customer service a new level of comfortability. It allows banks to meet customers' expectations with comprehensive digital support. With Artificial Intelligence, you can achieve greater precision and accuracy. From cash transfer to bills payment, cards management, and other support, AI can significantly enrich the satisfaction level of your customers. All of these operations can be easily managed through desktops, smartphones, and other mobile devices.

Scam Recognition

With an immense growth of banking fraud, scam recognition and reduction has become challenging for the banking sector. Several banks tried to identify the factors and powerful solutions but couldn't succeed. However, AI makes it easier to detect the factors involved in frauds and support investigators. It improves financial security with advanced fraud prevention tactics. Artificial Intelligence works as a real-time scam solution for the banking sector while handling complex situations and tactics. Based on advanced data crunching, AI can detect fraud by flagging unusual transactions. It also feeds back into the consumer's profile which subsequently builds a secure environment.

Advanced Data Analytics

One of the main advantages of AI is its ability to complete tedious tasks through intricate automation, resulting in better productivity. Based on a machine learning algorithm, AI can quickly consume and process a massive amount of data at an expedited level. The enormous speed brings efficiency to financial services, providing scope for personalized offerings to consumers. What's even more, AI makes faster decisions while carrying out actions quickly. With such advantages, it is nearly obvious that the majority of banks and financial institutions will adopt AI to stay competitive and deliver better customer support. However, several cons are also associated with a machine learning algorithm. As it continues to learn and grow, the decision-making capabilities may create problems in the near future.

Disadvanages of AI in Banking Sector

Artificial intelligence is also expected to massively disrupt banks and traditional financial services. Some of its disadvantages are listed below.

Highly Expensive

Production and maintenance of artificial intelligence demand huge costs since they are very complex machines. AI also consists of advanced software programs which require regular updates to meet the needs of the changing environment. In the case of critical failures, the procedure to reinstate the system and recover lost codes may require enormous time and cost.

Bad Calls

Though Artificial Intelligence can learn and improve, it still can't make judgment calls. Humans can take individual circumstances and judgment calls into account when making decisions, something that AI might never be able to do. Replacing adaptive human behavior with AI may cause irrational behavior within ecosystems of humans and things.

Distribution of Power

There is a constant fear of AI superseding or taking over the humans. Artificial intelligence can give a lot of power to the few individuals who are controlling it. Hence, AI carries the risk and takes control away from humans while dehumanizing actions in several ways.

Unemployment

Replacement of the workforce with machines can lead to wide-reaching unemployment. Moreover, if the use of AI becomes rampant, people will be highly dependent on the machines and lose their creative power. Unemployment is a socially undesirable issue. Individuals with nothing to do can lead to the devastating use of their minds. Be it banking or any other sector; Artificial intelligence can effectively increase the unemployment rate.

Artificial Intelligence delivered to wrong hands can turn out to be a serious threat to humankind. If individuals start thinking destructively, they can generate havoc with these advanced machines. The challenges introduced by the emergence of artificial intelligence revolve around several things. However, AI is a right balance of skill and emotions which is continually growing. Artificial intelligence provides banks, financial institutions, and tech companies with significant competitive advantages. Nevertheless, it can completely transform the financial sector and make it faster, but this will only be possible if the financial industry can manage the security risk of systems based on AI.

What does artificial intelligence mean for the bank service office workers?

With all these new artificial intelligence use cases comes the question of whether machines will force humans into obsolescence. The jury is still out: Some experts vehemently deny that artificial intelligence will automate so many jobs that millions of people find themselves unemployed, while other experts see it as a pressing problem.

"The structure of the workforce is changing, but I don't think artificial intelligence is essentially replacing jobs in bank service working environment. It allows us to really create a knowledge-based economy and leverage that to create better automation for a better form of life. It might be a little bit theoretical, but I think if you have to worry about artificial intelligence and robots replacing some bank service jobs, e.g. bank security, bank enquiry service,. But, AI can not replace bank counter service staffs to do saving or withdrawing money transfer tasks when any customers prepare to save money or withdraw money in bank counters. As this technology develops, the AI bank service will see new startups, numerous saving or withdraw transactions from consumer won't be raise more easily.

AI to Banking and Finance industry

The banking and finance industry plays a major role in our lives. I mean the world runs on money and banks are essentially the gatekeepers that regulate that flow. Did you know that the banking and finance industry heavily relies on artificial intelligence for things like customer service, fraud protection, investment, and more? A simple example is the automated emails that you receive from banks whenever you do an out of the ordinary transaction. Well, that's AI watching over your account and trying to warn you of any fraud.

AI is also being trained to look at large samples of fraud data and find a pattern so that you can be warned before it happens to you. Also, when you hitch a little snag and chat with bank's customer service, chances are that you are chatting with an AI bot. Even the big players in the finance industry use AI to analyze data to find the best avenues to invest money so they can get the most returns with the least risk. That's not all, AI is poised to play an even bigger role in the industry as major banks across the world are investing billions of dollars in the AI technology and we all will observe its effects sooner than later

How AI influences our daily working life in any office working environment Can AI bring only disadvantages? If AI can bring disadvantges, what are its disadvantages to any working environment ?The entire tech world is debating the consequences of artificial intelligence and the part AI is going to play in shaping our future. While we might think that artificial intelligence is at least a few years away from causing any considerable effects on our lives, the fact remains that it is already having an enormous impact on us. Artificial intelligence is affecting our decisions and our lifestyles every day. Don't believe me? I shall indicate some product examples how AI anticipates which can influence our working culture in any office environment.

Examples of how Artificial Intelligence assistance to office working environment may include as below:

1. Smartphones

Smartphones have become the most indispensable tech product that we own today and we use it almost all the time. Well, if you are using a smartphone, you are interacting with AI whether you know it or not. From the obvious AI features such as the built-in smart assistants to not so obvious ones such as the portrait mode in the camera, AI is impacting our lives in every day office working environment.

In fact, the two examples that I provided that our working world of AI and how it is effecting our working lives. Firstly, there are the obvious AI elements which most of us have some knowledge about. For example, when you are using a smart assistant in office, whether it's Google Assistant, Alexa, Siri, or Bixby, you more or less know that these assistants are based on AI. However, when we are using a feature such as the portrait mode effect while shooting a picture, we never consider that AI might be behind that too. Have you ever thought how the Google Pixel phones or iPhones can capture such great portrait shots? The answer is artificial intelligence. So, when any office workers need to find any knowledge to solve their working problem immediately in any offices. They may apply AI smart phone tools to help them to apply online channel to search any new knowledge to attempt to solve their working problem in possible, when their computers have none any computers in offices.

Now more and more manufacturers are including AI in their smartphones with big chip manufacturers including Qualcomm and Huawei producing chips with built-in AI capabilities. The AI integration is helping in bringing features like scene detection, mixed and virtual reality elements, and more. AI is going to play an even major role in the coming years. We are already seeing the huge emphasis on AI with the latest Android and iOS updates. Features like app actions, splices, and adaptive battery in Android Pie and Siri shortcut and Siri suggestions in iOS 12 are made possible with AI. So, next time if any office workers think AI is not effecting them, take out your smartphone to replace computers to find any knowledge to help you to solve any tasks problems immediately in offices.

2. Social Media Feeds

If you are thinking that smart cars don't personally effect you as they are still not in your country or city, well, how about something which you use on a daily basis. Even if you are living under a rock, there's a high probability that you are tweeting from underneath it. If Twitter's not your choice of poison, maybe it's Facebook or Instagram, or Snapchat or any of the myriad of social media apps out there. Well, if you are using social media, most of your decisions are being impacted by artificial intelligence. So, any office workers may apply AI to help them to gather any new information to solve any difficult task problems , if their managers can not assist them to solve any sudden tasks problem, they are encountering to need to solve any working complex tasks problem internet social media in any any office working environment immediately.

From the feeds that office staffs can see in their working timeline to the notifications that you receive from these apps, everything is curated by AI. AI takes all your past behavior, web searches, interactions, and everything else that you do when you are on these websites and tailors the experience just for you. The sole purpose of AI here is to make the apps so addictive that you come back to them again and again, and I am ready to place a bet that

AI is winning this war against you.

3. Online Ads Network

One of the biggest users of artificial intelligence is the online ad industry which uses AI to not only track user statistics but also serve us ads based on those statistics. Without AI, the online ad industry will just fail as it would show random ads to users with no connection to their preferences what so ever. AI has become so successful in determining our interests and serving us ads that the global digital ad industry has crossed 250 billion US dollars with the industry projected to cross the 300 billion mark in 2019. So next time when any product developers are going online and seeing ads or product recommendation, know that AI is impacting to any new products advertisement method more efficiently.

4. AI can be any office security

While we can all debate the ethics of using a broad surveillance system, there's no denying the fact that it is being used and AI is playing a big part in that. It is not possible for humans to keep monitoring multiple monitors with feeds from hundreds if not thousands of cameras at the same time, and hence, using AI makes perfect sense. With technologies like object recognition and facial recognition getting better and better every day, it won't be long when all the security camera feeds are being monitored by an AI and not a human. While there's still time before AI can be fully implemented such as security in any offices, this is going to be our future.

5. Smart Keyboard Apps

Smart Keyboard Apps. Granted, not everyone loves dealing with on-screen keyboards. However, they have become far more intuitive, allowing users to type comfortably and faster. What has probably proved to be a catalyst for them is the integration of AI. The smart keyboard apps keep a tab on the writing style of a user and predict words and emojis accordingly. Thus, typing on the touchscreen has become faster and more convenient. Not to mention, artificial intelligence also plays a vital role in pin-pointing misspellings and typos. So, any office workers can apply smart keyboard apps to help their to raise typing efficiency and reduce wrong typing word in error when they need to type any document in offices.

6. E-Commerce

` AI-driven algorithms have kind of given the much-needed impetus to e-commerce to provide a more personalized experience. According to several reports, its usage has vastly increased sales and also played a good part in building loyal relationships with customers. Thus, companies take advantage of AI to deploy chatbots to collect pivotal data and also predict purchases to create a customer-centric experience. Yet to come across this shift of strategy? Just spend some time with sites like Amazon and eBay and you will soon get to know how fast the landscape is changing around you – for the better! So, Ai can help any businesses to achieve e-commerce sale channel more easily.

7. Smart Email Apps

In any office working environment, if you still find your inbox cluttered with too many unwanted messages, chances are pretty high that you are still stuck with an old school email app. You heard it right! Modern email apps like Spark make the most of AI to get rid of spam messages and also categorize emails so that you can quickly access the important ones. What's more, they also offer smart replies based on the messages you receive to help you reply to any email quickly. The "Smart Reply" feature of Gmail is a great example of this. It uses AI to scan the text of the email and provides you with contextual answers. So, AI can help any office staffs to know who had sent any message from email and respond their email immediate , when AI can help any offices to avoid to receive any email spam rubbish email message in any time, even after working hours, it means that AI is working to help any office staffs to avoid to receive any email spam rubblish message in any time. So, when they go to office to work, even they go home after working hours. They can know whether what the important email messages are sent to their office email in boxes any time. Then, they can send email to respond their customers' enquires any time. So, AI can help any office workers can have chance to work at homes.

The Future of Artificial Intelligence In The Workplace

Smart technologies aren't just changing our homes; they're edging their way into their numerous industries and are disrupting the workplace. Artificial Intelligence (AI) has the potential to improve productivity, efficiency and accuracy across an organization – but is this entirely beneficial? Many fear that the rise of AI will lead to machines and robots replacing human workers and view this progression in technology as threat rather than a tool to better ourselves.

With AI continuing to be a prominent buzzword in 2019, businesses need to realize that self-learning and black-box capabilities are not the panacea. Many organisations are already beginning to see the incredible capabilities of AI, using these advantages to enhance human intelligence and gain real value from their data. As there is increasing evidence demonstrating the benefits of intelligent systems, more decision-makers in the boardroom are gaining a better understanding of what AI can really offer. Research conducted by EY explains "organizations enabling AI at the enterprise level are increasing operational efficiency, making faster, more informed decisions and innovating new products and services."

Today In: Cybersecurity

The first companies employing AI systems across the board will gain competitive advantage, reduce cost of operations and remove head counts. Whilst this may be a positive from a business perspective, it is obvious why this a worry for those working in roles at risk of displacement. The introduction of these technologies will likely trigger an issue with unions and job security due to the substantial operational changes. Although AI will affect every sector in some way, not every job is at equal risk. PwC predicts a relatively low displacement of jobs (around 3%) in the first wave of automation, but this could dramatically increase up to 30% by the mid-2030's. Occupations within the transport industry could potentially be at much greater risk, whereas jobs requiring social, emotional and literary abilities are at the lowest risk of displacement.

A positive future with artificial intelligence

Many businesses and individuals are optimistic that this AI-driven shift in the workplace will result in more jobs being created than lost. As we develop innovative technologies, AI will have a positive impact on our economy by creating jobs that require the skill set to implement new systems. 80% of respondents in the EY survey said it was the lack of these skills that was the biggest challenge when employing AI programs. It is likely that artificial intelligence will soon replace jobs involving repetitive or basic problem-solving tasks, and even go beyond current human capability. AI systems will be making decisions instead of humans in industrial settings, customer service roles and within financial institutions. Automated decisioning will be responsible for tasks such as approving loans, deciding whether a customer should be onboarded or identifying corruption and financial crime. Organisations will benefit from an increase in productivity as a result of greater automation, meaning more revenue will generated. This thus provides additional money to spend on supporting jobs in the services sector.

How to take advantage of AI to any offices

Due to the vast array of jobs that could be impacted by AI, it is fundamental to address the potential pitfalls of these technologies. Business need to overcome the trust and bias issues surrounding AI by achieving an effective and successful implementation that makes it possible for everyone to benefit. Governments must ensure that gains from AI are shared widely across society to prevent social inequality between those affected and unaffected by these developments. For example, this could be through increased investment into training.With the additional cost-savings from implementing AI systems, employers should also focus on upskilling their current employees.

To properly leverage the power of AI, we need to address the issue at an educational level, as well as in business. Education systems needs to focus on training students in roles directly associated to working with AI, including programmers and data analysts. This requires more emphasis to be put on STEM subjects (science, technology, engineering and mathematics). Also, subjects centered around building creative, social and emotional skills should be encouraged. Whilst artificial intelligence will be more productive than human workers for repetitive tasks, humans will always outperform machines in jobs requiring relationship-building and imagination. Artificial intelligence will change our world both inside and outside the workplace. Instead of focusing on the fear surrounding automation, businesses need to embrace these new technologies to ensure they implement the most effective AI systems to enhance and compliment human intelligence

How AI can help office workers to do tasks more easily

Companies are currently spending big on artificial intelligence and machine learning initiatives to the tune of $12 billion, but estimates put that figure as high as $57.6 billion by 2021, according to the International Data Corporation (IDC). With such massive shifts, the focus is usually on what we might lose, but it shouldn't be. A recent report on the future of work from the McKinsey Global Institute suggests that while only about 5% of jobs can be completely eliminated by automation, the rise of AI requires workers to beef up both technical and soft skills in order to stay competitive.

What's seldom discussed is how AI can revolutionize our jobs. It's now possible to pinpoint peak productivity for a single day, improve communication in meetings (even before people ever work together face to face), or even teach you to be a better leader, all thanks to AI platforms. I shall indicate these advantages to bring any office benefits from AI assistance as below:

1. AI can help any companies to get better to hire the best applicants
AI has the greatest potential to change the way companies find candidates, according to Alexander Rinke, cofounder and CEO of Celonis. The company's process-mining technology helps businesses to understand the areas where automation can help humans, he says. In HR departments, Celonis can help identify how fast workers come and go, the cost per hire, and which positions take the longest to fill. AI helped enable one customer's ability to identify bottlenecks in recruitment and reduced process costs internally by 30% as well as get them hired more quickly, he says.
Crafting a resume has never been easier, nor has landing an interview. Another example is how recruitment software provider iCIMS, in partnership with Google, is helping job seekers find jobs directly through the search engine, thanks to Google's AI and machine learning capabilities. Susan Vitale, iCIMS's chief marketing officer says that in addition to reducing the number of expired job postings, machine learning is underlying a private beta program of Google's Cloud Jobs Discovery model. "For a candidate searching for, say, a CTO role, Cloud Job Discovery will serve up CTO positions as well as jobs with titles that are similar, but not verbatim, such as chief technology officer or chief technical officer," says Vitale. This model also allows for conceptual search results, such as serving up job listings for cashiers, sales associates, and store associates when someone searches for one versus just only showing jobs that exactly match the keyword search criteria, she adds.

2. AI can help any office workers to raise much more productive efficiencies
John Furneaux, CEO and cofounder of Hive, says predictive analytics will help us better understand how we work. "It can tell us just about everything we want to know about teams and collaboration, for example, if men or women get more done in the afternoon, and if summer Fridays are a myth," he says. (Everyone thinks summer Fridays aren't productive, but in reality there's no difference between those and other Fridays during the year–productivity is equally low.)
Using a data set of over 30,000 completed actions across Hive workspaces, Furneaux says they were able to identify some notable trends in productivity. For example, men were far more productive early in the day, with a sharp decline in the afternoon, while women had a slower start to the day but were far more productive in later hours than their male counterparts. And analyzing chat messages revealed that women appear to

complete more tasks when chatting, suggesting they use communication as a key tool to completing work. Similarly, Nintex Hawkeye analyzes data on business processes by types, users, roles, and departments to see who's doing the work and how long it takes them to do it. Management can monitor and analyze those metrics in real time.

3. AI can help any managers to make the most fair compensation and eliminate wage gaps to every staffs

Tanya Jansen, cofounder of the compensation management platform beqom, says that AI and predictive analytics can eliminate unconscious bias from compensation. Jansen says that AI based on a variety of rules including education, experience, certifications, and more can make compensation more fair and help businesses move closer to closing pay gaps. "Specifically, AI can help solve gender pay gaps and the CEO-to-worker pay gap, in which pay ratios of Fortune 500 companies range from 2:1 at the low end to nearly 5000:1 at the high end," she says. Additionally, the use of AI-driven compensation technology to make pay more fair can mitigate the risk of employee turnover, which costs businesses as much as 33% of a worker's annual salary to replace them.

4. AI can help any office staffs to arrange better meetings

Augmented Reality (AR) is still in its infancy, but AI and machine learning are the core components that make it work. As such, Christa Manning, the vice president and solution provider research leader at Bersin, Deloitte Consulting LLP, says that AR can help workers find the right information, in the right place, at the right time to make the best decisions wherever they may be working. For example, as more companies adopt video meetings and collaborative workspaces, it's likely we'll begin to see HR-curated information like talent profiles and work styles layered over interactions through AR."Imagine being in a video conference with a colleague and having direct insight into their communication style, seeing tips on how to best interact with them or reminders of what needs to be discussed. SO, AI can help any organizations to conclude or find the best methods to solve any problems after their every discussion in any meetings.

How AI is improving onboarding and training. AI coaching tools first learn by observing how different employees conduct specific tasks. Then these tools can walk new employees through how to complete those tasks—or even coach existing employees on how to do things more effectively or efficiently. Chorus is a great example of this technology. It analyzes sales calls while they happen, offering tips to help sales reps manage the cadence of meetings and use the most effective messaging. It also records all sales calls and compiles statistics for each sales rep, providing everyone with the tools they need to help them close more deals and conduct more effective calls. Another example is Cogito, a tool that combines AI with behavioral science to help customer service employees provide better phone support. It monitors calls for voice signals, providing real-time suggestions to representatives on how to improve the conversation.

5. AI can help any managers to be better leaders

Indiggo, a platform powered by a proprietary AI tool called "indi," functions as a brain that has consumed all the knowledge the company has gathered in its 15 years of operation. It also uses an algorithm to provide an estimate of how much time is wasted by a company by analyzing the size of its management team. Then it taps their calendars to see how they spend their time, and walks individual managers through a type of Q&A to make sure they are clear on what their top three priorities are, and how that relates to the organization's priorities, which will indicate if that strategy is moving forward or not. "The counterintuitive impact of these advances is that they actually make human work truly irreplaceable," Alexander Rinke, the cofounder and CEO of Celonis says. As such, he reminds us, "Humans are much better at processes that involve reasoning, judgment, and interaction with people." So, AI can recommend more accurate and useful opinions to help any managers to solve their managing challenges in office any time.

How AI is eliminating repetitive administrative tasks

There are a lot of tasks that knowledge workers spend time on that provide little—if any—value.For example, say you need to schedule a meeting to get consensus on a decision before moving forward, but you need five people to join the meeting. It's easy to spend a ton of time sending email back-and-forth or finding an open slot on everyone's calendar.That's not the most rewarding use of your time for you or your company.Tools like X.ai give employees AI-powered personal assistants that perform administrative tasks like scheduling, rescheduling, and cancelling meetings.

How AI is transforming internal communications and support

Personnel on the teams that provide employee support have their hands full with other responsibilities, too. HR teams work on building the kind of company people love working for. IT maintains the company's network and keeps data secure. Office managers frequently run big events like holiday parties.These tasks are crucial, but they're often hard for teams to focus on because they're busy answering routine questions. AI service desks like askSpoke allow employee support teams to balance their service commitments with other important responsibilities by reducing interruptions from rote, repetitive requests.Employees can askSpoke for whatever they need over Slack, email, SMS, and the web. askSpoke's friendly AI will automatically provide a prompt response.

How AI is transforming marketing, sales, and customer service

AI-powered chatbots help with external support as well. Just like with internal support tools like askSpoke, these chatbots learn from real marketers, salespeople, and customer service reps and are eventually able to answer questions as accurately as a knowledgeable person.For example, chatbot for Messenger helps customers plan their vacations. It books flights, hotels, and cars, highlights destination attractions, and even provides answers to questions like "Where can I go for $100 expense budget only?"

How AI is transforming business data and analytics

It's hard to run a competitive business today without data. But even massive amounts of data are useless without a way to transform that data into valuable insights. That's typically why you'd want to hire a data scientist—which just happens to be one of the most difficult roles to fill. How AI is fighting fraud and transforming security. Have you ever taken a call from your bank to find that someone used your debit card fraudulently? Most likely, your bank used some form of AI to detect the fraudulent transaction and decline it. Applying the same basic technology to the workplace helps identify security risks and keeps customer, employee, and company data safe. AI-powered software can automatically detect and address threats among thousands or millions of signals that humans would never be able to parse (especially not in real-time).

How AI is transforming productivity

While AI is transforming the workplace in many different ways across every industry, it's impacting productivity most of all. When your office staffs don't have to scroll through calendars to look for open meeting times, build reports in spreadsheets to look for insights, or spend your day answering the same questions over and over again, you're more productive. Workers are freed from redundant and mindless tasks, giving them more time to do work that matters, solve problems, and exercise their creativity. Some tools use AI to specifically monitor and boost productivity. For example, Deloitte's LaborWise provides company leaders and managers with productivity analytics that help them identify areas where labor costs are too high, impediments that slow people down, and departments that need additional staff.

In conclusion, what AI means for the workplace of the future. While some will dramatize the negative impacts of AI, cognitive computing, and robotics, these powerful tools will also help create new jobs, boost productivity, and allow workers to focus on the human aspects of work. Essentially, automation frees companies and their employees up to be more empathetic, to focus on things like the customer experience, employee engagement, and workplace culture.

What are traditional office tools to be replaced by AI ?

Artificial intelligence (AI) is predicted to eliminate over a million jobs in the next few years, potentially replacing lower level positions like administrative assistants with humanoid robots or voice assistants. But in the nearer future, fresh AI-driven software and products are also moving to eliminate non-human elements of the workplace by replacing traditional office tools, including both physical products and everyday electronic processes. Why should businesses switch from the tried-and-true to emerging technology? Many of the experts TechRepublic talked to said the AI options streamline business practices, making their adopters work smarter instead of harder. I shall indicate these office tools ,they can be applied to help any office staffs to finish their these tasks in office, they may include as below:

1. Scheduling

Workloud's end-to-end, cloud-based workforce management software takes scheduling from paper or Excel and moves it to the cloud. Everything from clocking in and out to monitoring employee absences is fully digitalized.Schedules and timesheets are accurate, created easily, and accessible through the service's web, tablet, and mobile apps. The software can also be used for absence management.

2. Employee talent selection

Using AI and organizational behavior science, can be used to replace internal spreadsheets and databases designed to monitor human capital. By mining employee attributes and experiences, the software can recommend who would be best for a project. The software also collects reviews after projects to better predict successful employee-project matches.The traditional hiring process is slow, biased and inaccurate, By removing humans from the beginning stages of the process, it can become faster and more fair, and result in better hires.

AI software automates the hiring process, using online simulations instead of manual screenings and interviews. Using the software, employers can include tasks in a job application, allowing job candidates to show technical skills that may be necessary for a job. Employers can't rule out candidates until they see how the candidate performs, eliminating bias that occurs in the resume reading stage. Both sides also automatically receive updates about each other's steps, reducing the amount of time it takes to .

3.Timesheets: Allocate

Using AI and machine learning, the software registers an employee's computer activity throughout the day. The data, which can also pull information from email and calendars, is used to suggest timesheet entries to reflect a more accurate amount of time an employee spent working. The employee can review and revise as necessary. However, the software doesn't spy on or monitor employees. The data is only available to each employee, while others in the company can only see the timesheet's output, which Allocate said would be the same information available if a manual sheet was used. So,replacing manual timesheets with Allocate has three advantages: More accurate time entry, project analytics, and "unsucking' the work experience."

4. Document storage

By using AI to read and analyze business and legal documents, AI can store all of the important document-based information in the cloud. The severe reduction in print-outs means less paper and ink, fewer products like binder clips and boxes to store and organize all of the paper, and more employee time freed up from not needing to manually sort through every document.

For example, in any lawyer offices, legal professionals' morale in the industry can suffer when they are pushed into performing such dull, repetitive tasks like sorting through and coding documents by hand, With AI tools to automate those duties, lawyers can focus on more meaningful projects and boost the business's and clients' success as a result. While focused on law firms, businesses that have a lot of unstructured data in documents may also be able to use the service to free up employee time and save on printing costs.

5. Scanners: Adobe Scan

While documents are moving to the cloud more and more, sometimes a physical copy of a document still needs to be scanned using a bulky office scanner. Adobe Scan, an app that condenses a scanner to the size of a smartphone, can rid offices of the need for an in-house scanner. Users can download and open the app, then hold their device over whatever they need to scan. Adobe Sensei then turns the scan into a PDF, and sends it to the Adobe Document Cloud. The app can transform any image into digital text that can then be searched and used electronically. The app streamlines the scanning process, making scans cleaner and more immediate. For businesses already using Adobe services, the app makes documents easily accessible.

6. Landline phones

While landlines in homes are increasingly less common, the same cannot be said for offices. But using chatbots and AI integrations, RingCentral is trying to replace traditional office landline phone systems. The platform offers over 100 integrations, including that AI landline phones can let employees check their voicemail, and a Gong.io option that listens to call recordings to find traits of successful employees than can be used in training. An add-on for Gmail lets users switch from emailing back and forth to a voice session without needing to look up contact information. AI landline phone is easy to adopt and use in the workplace, and is more customizable than standard phone systems, said David Lee, vice president of platform products. Compared to the traditional option, the cloud-based option is "future-proof.

How artificial intelligence can raise office efficiency

Artificial Intelligence is already impacting every industry through automation and machine learning, bringing concerns that AI is on the fast track to replacing many jobs. But these fears aren't new, says Dan Jackson, director of Enterprise Technology at Crestron, a company that designs workplace technology. "I'd argue this is no different than when we moved from an agricultural to an industrial economy at the turn of the last century. The percentage of people working in agriculture significantly decreased, and it was a big shift, but we still have plenty of jobs 100 years later," he says. Anytime society experiences a major technological advancement, we need to be prepared for it to change the way we live and work. It's hard to imagine what the future of jobs will look like with AI, but that future exists. And optimists suggest that, like the sewing machine to the textile industry, AI will make us better, more efficient and faster workers.

In fact, many experts agree that AI has the potential to eliminate mundane, administrative work, while we will always rely on human workers to be empathetic, collaborative, creative and strategic. But it's impact on any industry lies in the hands of the business leaders who are responsible for adopting AI strategies.

● Training presents challenges

A recent study of 1,000 global companies by Accenture found that AI is already creating three new categories of jobs: trainers, explainers and sustainers. Trainers are the people who teach AI systems how to act -- whether it's language, human behavior or the intricacies of human interaction. Explainers are the liaison between technology and business leaders, providing more insight and clarity into machine learning for the non-tech workers. Sustainers are the workers required to maintain AI systems and troubleshoot any potential issues. Some jobs were highly technical and required advanced degrees, but other roles demanded innately human things such as empathy and interaction. Downstream jobs, such as those in sales, marketing, or service will change to take advantage of the insights from AI, but many of the core skills will remain. However, it might sound like any job related to AI will require years of technical knowledge, but that isn't the case. We've already seen a shift in tech hiring -- companies often need highly specific skill sets that are hard to find in potential candidates. As a result, more businesses are hiring employees with the right soft skills, and then training them in technical skills.

An office effort measured approach to AI

The real takeaway is that any approach to AI will need to consider the human aspect of every business. AI has great potential to increase efficiency and accuracy and it's already been proven in certain industries. For example, the use of AI In banking to identify and money laundering schemes. It's also improved healthcare by "increasing the speed and accuracy" of cancer diagnosistics. AI can also help reduce the cost and length of human trafficking investigations, a situation where time is precious. In these examples, AI hasn't replaced jobs, but has positively impacted efficiency.

Thus, we need to ensure our education system responds to equip young people with the appropriate skills and adaptability, while businesses and public organizations must invest in training. Perhaps most of all, we need to encourage imagination and willingness to experiment. The organizations that can innovate with AI will reap the benefits. Their growth will make them the primary source of future jobs. Companies have a choice when implementing AI. They can choose to effectively implement systems that make employee's lives easier and find creative ways to leverage the technology. It's up to employers to ease fears for workers around AI and build strategies that benefit everyone. Hence, some AI experts believe AI can only raise efficiency to some office tasks, however, AI can not still raise efficiency to all office tasks for any office deparments. The reasons are because some office tasks which can only dominate to finish by human office workers. These office tasks are as below:

How can leaders and managers improve employee productivity while still saving time? These below tasks, AI experts ensure that AI can not help any office workers to raise their efficiencies as below:

1. Office managers can not delegate to AI to help them to do. While this tip might seem the most obvious, it is often the most difficult to put into practice. We get it–your company is your baby, so you want to have a direct hand in everything that goes on with it. While there is nothing wrong with prioritizing quality (it is what makes a business successful, after all), checking over every small detail yourself rather than delegating can waste everyone's valuable time. Instead, give responsibilities to qualified employees, and trust that they will perform the tasks well. This gives your employees the opportunity to gain skills and leadership experience that will ultimately benefit your company. You hired them for a reason, now give them a chance to prove you right.

2. Office managers can not match Tasks to Skills to AI. Knowing your employees' skills and behavioral styles is essential for maximizing efficiency. For example, an extroverted, creative, out-of-the-box thinker is probably a great person to pitch ideas to clients. However, they might struggle if they are given a more rule-intensive, detail-oriented task. Asking your employees to be great at everything just isn't efficient–instead, before giving an employee an assignment, ask yourself: is this the person best suited to perform this task? If not, find someone else whose skills and styles match your needs.

3. Office managers can not teach AI to replace them how to communicate and teach their low level staffs how to work effectively. Every manager knows that communication is the key to a productive workforce. Technology has allowed us to contact each other with the mere click of a button (or should we say, tap of a touch screen)–this naturally means that current communication methods are as efficient as possible, right? Not necessarily. A McKinsey study found that emails can take up nearly 28% of an employee's time. In fact, email was revealed to be the second most time-consuming activity for workers (after their job-specific tasks). Instead of relying solely on email, try social networking tools (such as Slack) designed for even quicker team communication. You can also encourage your employees to occasionally adopt a more antiquated form of

contact...voice-to-voice communication. Having a quick meeting or phone call can settle a matter that might have taken hours of back-and-forth emails. All of above communication tasks, I believe that AI can not do better than managers in offices.

4. AI can not keep Goals Clear and focused to be better than managers. You can't expect employees to be efficient if they don't have a focused goal to aim for. If a goal is not clearly defined and actually achievable, employees will be less productive. So, try to make sure employees' assignments are as clear and narrow as possible. Let them know exactly what you expect of them, and tell them specifically what impact this assignment will have. One way to do this is to make sure your goals are "SMART" – specific, measurable, attainable, realistic, and timely. Before assigning an employee a task, ask yourself if it fits each of these requirements. If not, ask yourself how the task can be tweaked to help your workers stay focused and efficient.

5. AI can not know how to incentivize Employees to work more efficiently. One of the best ways to encourage employees to be more efficient is to actually give them a reason to do so. Recognizing your workers for a job well done will make them feel appreciated and encourage them to continue increasing their productivity. When deciding how to reward efficient employees, make sure you take into account their individual needs or preferences. For example, one employee might appreciate public recognition, while another would prefer a private "thank you." In addition to simple words of gratitude, here are a few incentives managers can know how to incentivize their staffs to work efficiently, but AI is only one machine, it can not perform very good.

6. AI does not know how to assist managers to train and Develop employees. Reducing training, or cutting it all together, might seem like a good way to save company time and money (learning on the job is said to be an effective way to train, after all). However, this could ultimately backfire. Forcing employees to learn their jobs on the fly can be extremely inefficient. So, instead of having workers haphazardly trying to accomplish a task with zero guidance, take the extra day to teach them the necessary skills to do their job. This way, they can set about accomplishing their tasks on their own, and your time won't be wasted down the road answering simple questions or correcting errors. Past their original training, encourage

continued employee development. Helping them expand their skillsets will build a much more advanced workforce, which will benefit your company in the long run. There are a number of ways you can support employee development: individual coaching, workshops, courses, seminars, shadowing or mentoring, or even just increasing their responsibilities. Offering these opportunities will give employees additional skills that allow them to improve their efficiency and productivity. But, AI do not know how to improve any office workers' performance more easily than managers.

● How can AI be dangerous to office working environment?

Most researchers agree that a superintelligent AI is unlikely to exhibit human emotions like love or hate, and that there is no reason to expect AI to become intentionally benevolent or malevolent. Instead, when considering how AI might become a risk to any office working environments, experts think two scenarios most likely:

The AI is programmed to do something devastating: Autonomous weapons are artificial intelligence systems that are programmed to kill. In the hands of the wrong person, these weapons could easily cause mass casualties. Moreover, an AI arms race could inadvertently lead to an AI war that also results in mass casualties. To avoid being thwarted by the enemy, these weapons would be designed to be extremely difficult to simply "turn off," so humans could plausibly lose control of such a situation. This risk is one that's present even with narrow AI, but grows as levels of AI intelligence and autonomy increase. So, if some businessmen apply AI to be business weapon to attack or steal their business competitors' business secret, e.g. contract document, employee performance report, profit report, even business secret document. Then, AI will be one business competitor weapon more than business assistant role in any business market. So, whether AI is office assistant or business competitor weapon, it depends on how the businessmen apply them to assist their business development.

The AI is programmed to do something beneficial, but it develops a destructive method for achieving its goal: This can happen whenever we fail to fully align the AI's goals with ours, which is strikingly difficult. If you ask an obedient intelligent car to take you to the airport as fast as possible, it might get you there chased by helicopters and covered in vomit, doing not what you wanted but literally what you asked for. If a superintelligent system is tasked with a ambitious geoengineering project, it might wreak havoc with our ecosystem as a side effect, and view human attempts to stop it as a threat to be met.

As these examples illustrate, the concern about advanced AI isn't malevolence but competence. A super-intelligent AI will be extremely good at accomplishing its goals, and if those goals aren't aligned with ours, we have a problem. You're probably not an evil ant-hater who steps on ants out of malice, but if you're in charge of a hydroelectric green energy project and there's an anthill in the region to be flooded, too bad for the ants. A key goal of AI safety research is to never place humanity in the position of those ants. Because AI has the potential to become more intelligent than any human, we have no surefire way of predicting how it will behave. We can't use past technological developments as much of a basis because we've never created anything that has the ability to, wittingly or unwittingly, outsmart us. The best example of what we could face may be our own evolution. People now control the planet, not because we're the strongest, fastest or biggest, but because we're the smartest. If we're no longer the smartest, are we assured to remain in control?

A captivating conversation is taking place about the future of artificial intelligence and what it will/should mean for humanity. There are fascinating controversies where the world's leading experts disagree, such as: AI's future impact on the job market; if/when human-level AI will be developed; whether this will lead to an intelligence explosion; and whether this is something we should welcome or fear. But there are also many examples of of boring pseudo-controversies caused by people misunderstanding and talking past each other. To help ourselves focus on the interesting controversies and open questions — and not on the misunderstandings — let's clear up some of the most common myths.

There have been a number of surveys asking AI researchers how many years from now they think we'll have human-level AI with at least 50% probability. All these surveys have the same conclusion: the world's leading experts disagree, so we simply don't know. For example, in such a poll of the AI researchers at the 2015 Puerto Rico AI conference, the average (median) answer was by year 2045, but some researchers guessed hundreds of years or more. There's also a related myth that people who worry about AI think it's only a few years away. In fact, most people on record worrying about superhuman AI guess it's still at least decades away. But they argue that as long as we're not 100% sure that it won't happen this century, it's smart to start safety research now to prepare for the eventuality. Many of the safety problems associated with human-level AI are so hard that they may take decades to solve. So, any businessmen ought have business moralty to know whether they ought how to apply their AI to assist their business development in our future office environment to be more moral.

● Five ways to use AI to improve business efficiency to these office tasks Regardless of a company's size or type, its executives typically look for ways to help it operate as efficiently as possible. They understand the link between efficiency and profitability. If employees waste too much time with drawn-out processes or complicated tasks, it'll be hard for the enterprise to remain profitable and adapt to challenges. Fortunately, artificial intelligence (AI) supports the need for effective business operations. Here are five ways enterprises can use AI for help: 5 ways to use AI to improve business efficiency image.Getting the best results from AI means looking at where bottlenecks exist, then figuring out if and how it might remove or minimise them. AI can help any offices to improve or raise efficiency to these tasks aspects as below:

1. Use AI to answer queries and support customer engagement
Chatbots are an increasingly popular option for businesses to try, and they use AI to work. Companies often build chatbots that can answer any questions from customers that come through outside of business hours. Some identify the nature of a person's problem, then either attempt to tackle it with preprogrammed answers or pass the communications to a human support worker. The retail industry, in particular, saw success by deploying chatbots. Global data collected by Juniper Research shows an estimated 2.6 billion retail-based chatbot interactions in 2019, and the company forecasts the number to rise to 22 billion in 2023.
Chatbots are excellent for answering simple questions like "How late are you open today?" or "Do you have gluten-free menu options?" Getting quick answers to queries like those increases the chances customers will choose to do business with one company over another. Equally importantly, when chatbots can give responses in a matter of seconds, there's no need for humans to stop what they're doing and address the questions.

2. To enhance reporting speed and accuracy
Company reports reveal things such as which products are selling the fastest and where they're most popular. They can also confirm the impacts of marketing campaigns on product sales, break down the costs of a new packaging choice or shipping method, and much more. However, as anyone that files reports knows, creating them is a painstaking task, and trying to rush through the process could cause mistakes. Some forward-thinking companies are combining AI with big data analytics. Doing this brings

better forecasts and takes some of the burdens off the people who prepare the reports. AI also helps conquer the inevitability of mistakes. Even the most careful people make blunders, often because of mental fatigue.

AI learns to spot patterns in data and gets smarter with time. This means reports get finished faster and contain more-reliable information. The reliability aspect is crucial, especially since recently published research indicated two-thirds of the senior executives polled had no confidence or trust in big data. Using AI does not mean companies can do without data scientists. However, depending on the technology allows them to reduce the uncertainty that may otherwise exist. It also prevents employees who work with a company's data from being asked to recheck the findings, even if they initially took appropriate precautions to ensure accuracy.

3. To improve data transfer speeds

Fast data transfers help AI technology work. Concerning some information-intensive applications like virtual reality (VR), any slow transmissions greatly interfere with the realism, and content immersion people should enjoy after strapping on a VR headset. As it turns out, AI can improve data transfer speeds, too. For example, services exist that boost speeds across any wide-area network (WAN). Users enjoy consistently accelerated rates regardless of the kind of information transferred. Some companies have solutions that can reduce WAN job times by up to 98%. These AI-driven options work particularly well when companies need to move information between data centres or cloud environments.

4. To assist the IT team with identifying genuine cyberthreats and anomalies

One of the ongoing challenges faced by IT teams of all sizes is to separate the true cyber threats from false alarms. The difficulties associated with categorising the two types may mean cybersecurity professionals waste time getting to the bottom of things that are ultimately nonissues. They might miss the actual threats that could derail a company's operations. Besides detecting possible intrusions associated with a network, AI can screen for software abnormalities that may make it easier for cybercriminals to orchestrate their attacks successfully. It can also find malicious software hackers installed. Due to this kind of information and the advantages of receiving it through real-time updates, IT security teams can work more productively. They can use the majority of their resources on the threats that matter most to the company's stability.

Some organisations have even used AI to help them conquer the substantial skills shortage in the cybersecurity industry. At Texas A&M University, the Security Operations Center deals with about a million attempted hacks each month. The facility has some full-time workers, but students comprise most of the staff. They work alongside AI that aids in threat monitoring, detection and remediation. Before students see possible threats, the smart technology finds and groups them. This approach saves time and lets the team get to work investigating the problems and deciding how to handle them.

5. To streamline the time-to-hire metric when filling new positions
Statistics show the average time required to hire a person for an open position ranges from 12.7 to 49 days, depending on the industry. The timing also varies based on the type of work a job requires. For example, it takes a shorter amount of time overall to find someone for an administrative or human resources position than one associated with a creative or advertising role. Then, of course, interviews are more extensive for high-profile work. Human resources professionals increasingly use AI to cut down on the time between first posting a job and finding the ideal individual to hire. For example, an AI platform could look for particular desired keywords in submitted resumes, saving hiring managers from poring over the documents themselves. AI can also pitch in during interviews. A company called VCV recently raised $1.7m to further develop its AI tool that has voice and facial recognition components. Candidates are asked to record videos of them answering interview questions, but they can't prepare for the specific content in advance.

In conclusion, AI Can Boost Efficiency at All Types of Companies. The examples here highlight why so many company leaders conclude that if they use AI, they could cut down on inefficiencies. Getting the best results from AI means looking at where bottlenecks exist, then figuring out if and how it might remove or minimise them. But, AI still lack enough effort to help all staffs to raise efficiency to all department tasks in any office environments.

● How the office energy Department is using AI to solve some of their office staffs electricity toughest challenges in their office working environment.

Insights from artifical intelligence has the potential to transform nearly every aspect of the world as we know it. Today, it is being applied to accelerate the pace of discovery in a wide variety of areas including energy, materials science, health care, national security, emergency response, transportation, and more. AI can be trained to help any energy department to gather data to avoid energy waste to be used to any organizations. So, AI is such as one super machine to do more accurate judgement to help any energy scientists to find the best methods to help any organizations to avoid to waste to use any energy daily. Then, organizations can avoid to spend too much energy to use in offices and they can save more money and avoid energy shortage challenge causes more easily. When the office managers can apply AI ability to reason and put it into a more automated format in a computer system to their every staffs' computer and record their computer electricity use record in their offices every day.

How can AI help offices to save energy or avoid to waste energy ?

The next industrial revolution is already happening. Artificial intelligence (AI) is ushering in an era of technologies that are faster, more adaptable, more efficient, and making the world more digitally connected. AI is best described as complementary to human intelligence, delivering the computing power to crunch numbers too big for people and recognize patterns too tedious for the human eye. In a Harvard Business Review study of 1,500 companies, it was found that the most significant performance improvements were made when humans and machines worked together. As AI becomes one of society's greatest assets, it's especially helpful for solving problems that seem larger than life — like protecting our natural environment.

Through machine learning, robotics, drones, and the internet of things (IoT), society can achieve better monitoring, understanding, and prevention of damage and stressors on Earth's land, air, and water. Even technology already available today could reduce energy usage in the U.S. by 12 to 22 percent, according to The Information Technology Industry Council (ITI). In the face of this dire reality, the potential of technology to help meet this challenge is a rare source of optimism. According to a recent survey by Intel and the research firm Concentrix, 74 percent of business-decision makers working in environmental sustainability agree artificial intelligence (AI) will help solve long-standing environmental challenges; 64 percent agree the Internet of Things (IoT) will help solve these challenges. As the field of AI develops, so will the potential to protect the environment. From the land and air to both drinking and ocean water, AI is shaping up to be the key that governments, organizations, and individuals can tap to work toward a cleaner planet, even AI can help offices to avoid to waste energy when staffs are working in offices every day.

Many AI scientists indicate that AI will also make renewable energy technology like solar panels and wind turbines more efficient and cost effective, helping them to become ubiquitous and lower society's dependence on fossil fuels. AI will also make renewable energy technology like solar panels and wind turbines more efficient and cost effective, helping them to become ubiquitous and lower society's dependence on the fossil fuels polluting the air — then hopefully eliminate them all together. Combined with the smart grid, another technology that will be enabled by AI, this will truly progress the way people receive and use electricity in their homes, offices, and everywhere else. Smart meters save energy by allowing for two-way communication between the grid and anything that uses electricity, giving energy providers a better understanding of usage and the ability to make real-time adjustments for efficiency. Customers will benefit from the real-time data too; seeing the increased costs at peak times will encourage them to voluntarily adjust their usage to save money. This will, in turn, save even more energy: a win-win. Plus, the process of delivering the energy itself will also be improved by the smart grid, thanks to Volt/VAR control systems that can reduce the amount of energy wasted when it's in electricity transmission lines.

Can AI replace office workers

Can AI replace all office workers to do their different tasks in office different department ? If AI can only replace some department office workers to do their simple tasks, how it can raise more efficiency to compare them in some business office environments. I shall indicate some office tasks to explain how AI can help these businesses to raise their efficiency in officesas below:

● AI insurance workers

Nowadays, some country offices begin apply robotics to replace human office workers in their companies. For example, Japanese company replaces office workers with artificial intelligence in insurance industry. A future in which human workers are replaced by machines is about to become a reality at an insurance firm in Japan, where more than 30 employees are being laid off and replaced with an artificial intelligence system that can calculate payouts to policyholders.

Fukoku Mutual Life Insurance believes it will increase productivity by 30% and see a return on its investment in less than two years. The firm said it would save about 140m yen (£1m) a year after the 200m yen (£1.4m) AI system is installed this month. Maintaining it will cost about 15m yen (£100k) a year. The move is unlikely to be welcomed, however, by 34 employees who will be made redundant by the end of March.

The system is based on IBM's Watson Explorer, which, according to the tech firm, possesses "cognitive technology that can think like a human", enabling it to "analyse and interpret all of your data, including unstructured text, images, audio and video".The technology will be able to read tens of thousands of medical certificates and factor in the length of hospital stays, medical histories and any surgical procedures before calculating payouts, according to the Mainichi Shimbun.

While the use of AI will drastically reduce the time needed to calculate Fukoku Mutual's payouts – which reportedly totalled 132,000 during the current financial year – the sums will not be paid until they have been approved by a member of staff, the newspaper said.

Japan's shrinking, ageing population, coupled with its prowess in robot technology, makes it a prime testing ground for AI. According to a 2015 report by the Nomura Research Institute, nearly half of all jobs in Japan could be performed by robots by 2035. For example, one Japan insurance company, Dai-Ichi Life Insurance has already introduced a Watson-based system to assess payments - although it has not cut staff numbers - and Japan Post Insurance is interested in introducing a similar setup, the Mainichi said. AI could soon be playing a role in the country's politics. Next month, the economy, trade and industry ministry will introduce AI on a trial basis to help civil servants draft answers for ministers during cabinet meetings and parliamentary sessions. The ministry hopes AI will help reduce the punishingly long hours bureaucrats spend preparing written answers for ministers.

● AI public service workers

The automated city: do we still need humans to run public services? If the experiment is a success, it could be adopted by other government agencies, according the Jiji news agency. If, for example a question is asked about energy-saving policies, the AI system will provide civil servants with the relevant data and a list of pertinent debating points based on past answers to similar questions.

The march of Japan's AI robots hasn't been entirely glitch-free, however. At the end of last year a team of researchers abandoned an attempt to develop a robot intelligent enough to pass the entrance exam for the prestigious Tokyo University. "AI is not good at answering the type of questions that require an ability to grasp meanings across a broad spectrum," Noriko Arai, a professor at the National Institute of Informatics, told Kyodo news agency. Hence, AI will have possible to replace some public service workers' tasks.

● AI replace warehouse workers

Denso's use of Drishti shows how some jobs will be transformed by artificial intelligence even when they're unlikely to be eliminated by AI anytime soon. Many jobs in manufacturing require dexterity and resourcefulness, for example, in ways that robots and software still can't match. But advances in AI and sensors are providing new ways to digitize manual labor. That gives managers new insights—and potentially leverage—on workers. For example,some workers say the results are unpleasant. Last year, Amazon warehouse employees in Minnesota staged a walkout to protest how the company uses inventory and worker-tracking technology. They allege that Amazon uses it to enforce a punishing working pace that causes injuries. The company has disputed those claims, saying it coaches employees on how to safely meet quotas.

Workers at Denso were initially wary of the prospect of being video-recorded all day to feed machine-learning algorithms, but Huffman says they have since come to appreciate Drishti's technology. After something goes wrong, workers can now look at the data and video with their managers, instead of having to hope bosses take their account of what happened seriously. Huffman says having a constant readout on productivity also helps managers be more responsive to nascent problems. "If somebody's struggling, not every associate is going to call for help," he says. "If we see their cycle time is jumping through the roof, we can go over and say 'Are you having any issues?'"Workers on Denso lines equipped with Drishti's technology now get a personal feed of their own data. Monitors on each workstation display how a worker is doing, says Raja Shembekar, a Denso vice president. If the worker completes their assembly step on time, they see a smiley face—if not, a frowny one. Hence, Amazon had begun to apply AI robotic to replace some warehouse workers' tasks.

For another factory manufacture working environment example, AI can replace many manufacture workers to do their tasks in factories. Route 9 skims by Boston and cuts clear across Massachusetts to Pittsfield, a city of roughly 50,000, the largest in Berkshire County. Well east of Pittsfield, Route 9 becomes Worcester Road, named for a city that in earlier times was the nation's largest manufacturer of wire—barbed wire, electrical wire, telephone wire and the wire used in the making of undergarments by the Royal Worcester Corset Co., once the largest employer of women in the United States. Older Worcester residents can still recall the factory bells pealing to signal the start and end of the workday. Now, the bells are silent, and the wire and corset factories have been replaced with three of the nation's largest employers: Walmart, Target and Home Depot. If this sounds familiar, it should. It has been nearly two decades since retail overtook manufacturing as the nation's most important job creator, employing roughly one of every 10 American workers—more people than in health care and construction combined. That's a lot of jobs.

Of course, not all retail jobs qualify as what most of us consider good jobs. Today, the average hourly wage for a nonsupervisory retail worker is $11.24, and less than half of retail workers receive benefits of any kind. Still, as a nation, we've come to a sort of uneasy peace with this trend. We know that manufacturing employs far fewer Americans today than it once did—that iPads and Macs aren't made in America and neither are many televisions, appliances, tools, toys or clothes. We also know that shopping for these appliances, tools, toys and clothes is an all-American pastime: On average, we spend nearly 45 minutes a day (more than 270 hours per year) purchasing goods and services. Retail has become the world as we know it, and many of us expect to make our living working in that world.Thanks to automation and a killer business model, Amazon is so efficient that it reaps nearly twice the revenue per employee of Walmart, despite the fact that Walmart, too, has a substantial online presence. Worldwide, Amazon has installed over 100,000 robots to labor in "perfect symbiosis" with humans in its warehouses and has plans to install many thousands more. While it's not clear what constitutes perfect symbiosis, the robots are said to save the company $22 million annually, per warehouse. The company's master plan of an autonomous future also includes goods delivered by drones and self-driving vehicles.

For while Amazon continues to open warehouses around the globe and staff them with many thousands of human beings, estimates are that every human on the Amazon payroll—whether full- or part-time—displaces two humans at traditional brick-and-mortar operations. And that's a feature, not a bug: As Tim Lindner, a veteran IT analyst, confided in a note to industry insiders, eradicating jobs is the explicit goal of any online retailer. As he once wrote: "Labor is the highest-cost factor in warehouse operations. It is no secret that Amazon is moving to highly automated operations within its distribution centers, and...it has additional technology that can further reduce the number of humans it needs to process customer orders.... You have heard the old programmer's phrase, 'Garbage in, garbage out.'... [With] the diminishing reading abilities of humans on the Receiving dock, finding an automated solution to eliminate the 'garbage in' problem is the holy grail. Amazon may have just patented it."

By garbage, Lindner meant human error, the alternative to which is apparently robotic precision. And robots can be very precise, especially when it comes to routine tasks. Sawyer, an industrial robot created by the former Boston-based Rethink Robotics, offers an impressive illustration of how all-embracing a robot arm can be. Sawyer is the brainchild of Rodney Brooks, the inventor of both Roomba, the robotic vacuum, and PackBot, the robot used to clear bunkers in Iraq and Afghanistan and at the World Trade Center after 9/11. Unlike Roomba and PackBot, Sawyer looks almost human—it has an animated flat-screen face and wheels where its legs should be. Simply grabbing and adjusting its monkey-like arm and guiding it through a series of motions "teaches" Sawyer whatever repeatable procedure one needs it to get done. The robot can sense and manipulate objects almost as quickly and as fluidly as a human and demands very little in return: While traditional industrial robots require costly engineers and programmers to write and debug their code, a high school dropout can learn to program Sawyer in less than five minutes. Brooks once estimated that, all told, Sawyer (and his older brother, the two-armed Baxter robot) would work for a "wage" equivalent of less than $4 an hour.

Robots loom large in discussions of work and its future, a conversation that can get mired in false assumptions. Until recently, many economists were skeptical that automation could permanently displace human workers on a large scale. People have always shifted away from work better done by machines, but the economic principle of "comparative advantage" predicts that humans will maintain an edge in many fields. Under this logic, technology will not displace us but set us free to do less dangerous, more challenging things, essentially the very things that make humans human. Of course, human workers are complicated. We get tired, hungry, distracted, angry, confused. We make mistakes, sometimes egregious ones. Machines lack our frailties and biases and are better equipped to weigh evidence fairly, without prejudice or false assumptions. Perhaps most critically, machines can retain and process data far more accurately than we can, and that data is growing exponentially.

Every minute of every day, Google services 3.6 million searches in the United States alone. Spammers send 100 million emails. Snapchatters send 527,000 photos, and the Weather Channel broadcasts 18 million forecasts. This and more data—properly collected, codified and analyzed—can be applied to automate almost any high-order task. Data can also serve as a surrogate for human experience and intuition. Online shopping and social media sites "learn" our preferences and use that information to make values-based assessments to influence our decisions and behavior. And, increasingly, machines excel in the tasks once thought uniquely human."Computers are able to see and hear, and have face-recognition capabilities that are significantly better than humans," says Vardi. "Machines understand the human world far better than they did just a few years ago. And we haven't discovered anything in the human brain that can't be modeled."

● AI can replace counter cashier service staffs

And robots need not be perfect, only equal to—or a tad better than—complicated and expensive humans. And technologists are working hard to make sure they are a tad better. For example, in the case of retail, it's become clear that many of us avoid the self-service checkout line—we prefer the cashier to punch in our purchases rather than do so ourselves. So it seems that the job of cashier—among the largest retail employment categories—is not directly at risk. But Zeynep Ton, an MIT management expert who focuses on the retail sector, says self-service checkout is only a first step and not a terribly smart one. "Customers recognized that self-service checkout is not an innovation, but merely a way of outsourcing the job to them, so they didn't like it," she says. "But new technology is coming that will make self-service checkout so much easier and faster, and that will have a real impact on retail employment."

Experts caution that the so-called apocalypse in retail predicted a few years ago has not yet come to pass. In fact, for every company closing existing stores, two more are opening new stores. Retail is a highly competitive industry, and technology is transforming not only the way we shop but the way we connect with brands—for example, just a few years ago, who would have imagined that Amazon would open actual retail stores? And while e-commerce has grown to 10 percent of retail, that still leaves 90 percent for brick-and-mortar stores. But those brick-and-mortar stores, too, are undergoing radical change that has serious implications for America's workforce.

As example, Lobaugh cites food trucks, which he says increasingly pose a threat to many fast-food outlets. Unlike restaurants pinned down by a pair of Golden Arches, food trucks are nimble—they can home in on areas where customers are most likely to gather at any particular time. They can also tailor their offerings to a particular region or even a neighborhood, as well as use Facebook or other media to get out the word on their menu items and locations. Small, specialty stores also have far more flexibility than large department stores. "Technology has reduced the cost of entry into new markets, so in retail there are fewer big, monolithic companies, but more small competitors," he says. "Companies are diversifying to meet the specific needs and desires of consumers—everyone's piece is getting smaller, but there are many more pieces."

But despite what it predicts will be a banner holiday season, this year Amazon took on far fewer seasonal employees than usual—100,000 employees versus 120,000 the previous two years. And while an Amazon spokeswoman insisted that automation is not a factor in this reduced workforce, others seem to not agree. In a recent report, Morgan Stanley analyst Brian Nowak soothed the fears of Amazon shareholders concerned with the wage increase by pointing out that automation had already and would continue to reduce the call for labor, and therefore reduce overall costs. When asked about this, Lobaugh again tactfully declined to comment—other than to say that while the retail sector had lost less ground than most people assume, retail employees were another matter. "There are winners," he says, "and then there are losers."

● AI can replace accountants in accountancy service industry

Not that long ago artificial intelligence (AI), robots and machine learning (ML) were thought to be things only found in science fiction films. Today, this type of technology is taking center stage in workplaces across the globe. Industries, including manufacturing, retail, agriculture, and customer service have already had AI replace some job positions that left workers scrambling to find new career options. This AI revolution is not expected to slow down anytime soon. In fact, experts anticipate that as many as 800 million jobs could be replaced with AI technology by the year 2030. Initially, AI technology and automation in the workplace seemed to only affect pink and blue-collar workers. As this technology advances and becomes more powerful, professional, white-collar workers, including accountants, are starting to worry about what the future holds for their career and if AI will be developed to own their professional skills in accounting service industry. In basic terms, AI technology is intelligent machines that are able to complete repetitive, mundane tasks at a fraction of the time it takes humans and with greater accuracy. The emergence of Machine Learning now allows AI platforms to observe, analyze and self-learn data and processes to improve its performance and accuracy over time. AI technology is already able to handle many accounting functions, such as tax preparation, payroll, and audits. Many of the leading accounting software providers, including Xero, Intuit and Sage have incorporated AI technology into their software to handle basic accounting tasks, such as bank reconciliations, invoice categorization, risk assessment, and audit processes, like expense submissions and invoice payments. Many of these standard tasks are extremely time-consuming, which has many accountants across the country worried about how the emerging AI technology will affect their billable hours. An even bigger concern is that AI technologies will replace the need for companies to work with accountants at all.

● AI Will Transform not Replace Accountants

While there is no doubt that AI technology is capable of handling many standard accounting tasks faster and more efficiently or that these capabilities will only increase over time, it doesn't mean the end for accountants. There always will be a need for that human element - human intelligence - at the other end of AI technology. In fact, according to leading research firm, Gartner, AI is set to create more jobs than it will replace, leaving workers, including accountants with options. Accountants don't have to worry about their job being replaced by AI any time in the near future. Companies will always need accountants that can analyze and interpret AI data, as well as provide consulting services. Rather than replacing the role of an accountant, AI technology will transform the duties an accountant performs.

With AI technology and machine learning handling many of the mundane, repetitive tasks, accountants will have more time to focus on other aspects of the job, such as consulting and data analysis. This is good news for many accountants. Rather than spending hours completing menial tasks, accountants of the future will be able to use and analyze AI data to provide their clients with sound business solutions.

In many ways, AI will help accountants improve their services. AI technology will improve data entry accuracy and lower the liability risk for accountants. In addition, emerging technology is more efficient at fraud detection, adding an extra layer of protection for accountants and their clients. It also provides real-time data, which allows accountants to provide real-time solutions. Even more impressive is the ability of machine learning to analyze large amounts of data instantly, evaluate past successes and failures in an effort to accurately predict future outcomes.

There is no way to escape the use of AI technology, at least not if you hope to remain competitive in the upcoming years. The speed, efficiency and accuracy of AI technology just cannot be beat. The only thing accountants can do is to embrace this new technology and learn how to maximize its use. The better equipped you are to help your clients integrate and utilize AI technology in their accounting processes the more valuable you will be. For example, many universities today are already incorporating IT and database management courses into their accounting program. This means that graduating students are coming into the workforce with the skills they need for future accounting work. Accountants already in the workforce must find ways to acquire these skills in order to remain relevant to their employers and/or their clients. Accountants can obtain the IT skills they need by attending seminars, using self-learning online programs or attending college-level courses. It is equally important for accountants to stay up-to-date on the latest accounting trends, emerging technologies and industry news. This will allows accountants to not only keep their jobs but to also provide more efficient services to their clients. Rather than worry about AI taking over their jobs, accountants should embrace this technology as a powerful solution to enhance customer services. Finally, accountants will be able to use all their training and experience to provide customer will real and effective business solutions, whether it's in reference to tax consulting, real estate deals, mergers, growth options, or any other business practice.

On conclusion, technology is advancing at record rates so now is the time to obtain the IT and database management skills you need to advance into the future. With the right skills and training, accountants are guaranteed a lucrative career that will last well into the future.

(AI) -driven automation industry development

5.1 (AI) - driven automation industry development how to influence work nature change

(AI) -driven automation industry will create wealth and expand economy growth to any countries, but it will be accompanied by changed in the skills that workers need to learn. One of main ways that technology increases productivity is by decreasing the number of labor hours needed to create a unit of output. It implies (AI) technology will influence low educated and low skillful labor number to be decreased (reduction employment number). In contrast, technological change tended to work in a different direction throughout the nowadays. The advance of computer and the internet raised the relative productivity of higher skilled workers. So, routine-intensive occupations that focused on predictable tasks disappearance, such as switch board, operators, filming checkers, travel agents and assembling line workers etc. were particularly replaced by new technologies.

However, today, it may be challenging to predict exactly which jobs will be most immediately affected by (AI) driven-automation. The reason is because (AI) is not a single technology, but rather a collection of technologies that are felt unevenly through the economy to influence job changing both negatively and positively. In positively view point, (AI) driven-automation will make many workers more productive and increase demand for certain skills. Consequently, new jobs are likely to be directly create in areas , such as the development and supervision of (AI) as well as indirectly created in a range of areas throughout the economy as higher incomes lead to expanded demand. Otherwise, in negatively view point, many traditional human needed (demand) skillful jobs will be threatened by automation are highly concentrated among lower-paid, lower-skilled and less -educated workers. It means automation will cause pressure on demand for this group, pressure and employment, if (AI) can replace the low skilled and less educated workers' jobs. Thus, (AI) will have negative influence to impact on the labor market.

(AI) capabilities will enable automation of some tasks that have long required human labor. Why can (AI) replace some simple human jobs? For example, advances in robotics are expanding machines' abilities to interact with and sharp the physical world. Combined , (AI) and robotics will give rise to smarter machines that can perform more sophisticated functions than ever before and brings more advantages that humans have exercised. This will permit automation of many tasks now performed by human workers and could change the shape of the labor market and human activity.

5.2 How (AI) influences labor market

Today, it may be challenging to predict exactly which jobs will be most immediately affected by (AI)-driven automation. Because (AI) is not a single technology, but rather a collection of technologies that are applied to specific tasks.

Some specific predictions are possible based on the current (AI) technology. For example, driving jobs and house cleaning jobs, bank counter service jobs, telephone enquiry service operators. Restaurant cooking jobs, simple accounting record service jobs etc. that require relatively less education to perform. Advancements in computer vision and related technologies have made the feasibility of fully appear more likely, potentially displacing some workers in driving-dominant professions. Seemingly similar robot, for which the operational tasks is less specific of navigating to a specific destination when following a set of given rules and preserving safety.

In the future, the effects of (AI) on the labor market in the decade ahead will continue the trend toward skill-biased change that computerization and communication innovations have driven in recent decades. Thus, some human driving occupation will be disappeared or replaced by (AI) automation driven. For example, bus drivers, light truck or delivery services drivers, heavy and tractor-trailer truck drivers, school drivers, tax drivers, travel bus drivers.

However, (AI) technology could enable some workers to focus time on other job responsibilities, boosting their productivity, and actually raised wage growth among those still holding the reshaped jobs. For example, salespeople, who currently spend a considerable amount of time driving could find themselves able to do other work when a car drives them from place to place, or inspectors and appraisers could fill out paperwork, when their car drives itself. This (AI) -driven technology should make these workers more productive, with (AI) -driven technology serving as a complement, not a substitute. New jobs will also likely be created, both in existing occupations cheaper transportation costs with lower prices and increase demand for products and all the related occupations, such as service and fulfillment, and in new occupations not currently foreseeable.

What kind of jobs will be created by (AI) technology? Predicting future job growth is extremely difficult, due to it depends on technologies or substitute for existing today as well as they may complement or substitute for existing human skills and jobs. However, (AI) will also lead to substantial indirect job creation to the degree it raises productivity and wages, it may also lead to higher consumption that would support additional jobs from high-end draft production to restaurant and retail. The future(AI) " augmented intelligence", the technology's role is as assisting and expanding the productivity of individuals rather than replacing human work. Thus, based on the biased-technical change framework, demand for labor will likely increase the most in the areas where humans complement (AI) automation technologies. For example, (AI) technology , such as IBM's Watson may improve early detection of some cancers or other illnesses, but a human healthcare professional is needed to work with patients to understand and translate patients' symptoms, inform patients of treatment options, and guide patients through treatment plans. Shipping companies may also partner workers who pick up and deliver products over the last feet with (AI) enabled autonomous vehicles that move workers efficiently from site to site. In such cases, (AI) augments what a human is able to do and allows individuals to either be move effective in their specially task or to operate on a larger scale. Thus, it seems (AI) technology will also create new jobs, raise productivities and workers' efficiencies.

Redefining management in
the workforce of artificial intelligence

● Change management

In the future, due to artificial intelligence influences to some kind of human jobs nature. So, the kind of human jobs of management methods will also need to change to adapt the artificial intelligence technology input to their organizations. It will cause challenges for every executive and manager if who won't have effort to manage their teams how to apply artificial intelligence technology to work efficiently and easily. For example, division of labor will change among humans and machines will increase. Thus, companies will have to adapt their training performance and talent strategies how to emphasize on work that how to make human judgment and skills and experimentation. Thus, (IA)'s greatest impact will be on administrative coordination and control tasks, such as scheduling , resource allocation.

In fact, mangers will encounter this challenges: How to apply human experience and expertise to judge critical business decisions and practices when the information available is insufficient to suggest a successful course of action? Due to this kind of work will require new skills and mindsets. I shall indicate these change management methods to adapt (AI) technology. Such as: administration and routine tasks, scheduling , allocation of resources and reporting will fall within the intelligence machines, responsibilities that have long been reserved for humans. For example, a typical store manager or a lead nurse at a nursing home most constantly arrange shift schedules, accounting for staff members' absences owing to illness, vacation time or sudden departures.

Thus, the managers need to learn how to arrange new division of labor within the organizations after (AI) technology had been implemented to the organization. Artificial intelligence is currently influencing into once considered exclusive to humans: assessing and acting on human emotions and personality traits. The influences to managers need to change their strategies to adapt (AI) technology implements include such as below:

Firstly, managers need to spend the bulk of their time on coordination and control tasks from intelligent system implements. Their time spending on these major three aspects from impact of intelligent system: coordinate and control, solve problems and collaborate and people and community , strategy and innovation three aspects. Thus (AI) will influence managers need to change their judgment method to teach whose teams how to adapt the (AI) system operations in any organizations.

Secondly, (AI) will influence top, middle and low level management needs to change to adapt the (AI) technology operations to any owned (AI) technology organizations in the future. Intelligent machines must be trained in context. Just like humans , on-the-job training is a requirement for such machines because they typically arrive with only very general capabilities. To get the most from (AI), managers at all levels must participate in the instructional experience and in the learning process and provides managers' familiarity with such systems on these aspects, e.g. How the system works and generate advice, how the system has a proven track record , how the system provides convincing explanations , how the system can make simple rule- based decisions.

Thirdly, managers need to learn how to make judgment more accurate (AI) systems assistance. Although (AI) will invariably take on more routine work and even augment human decision-making, it won't judgment work, the application of human experience and expertise to critical business decisions when the information available is insufficient to suggest a successful course of action or reliable enough to suggest an obvious course of action. For a sense of the nature of judgment work, consider big data marketing and sales analytics. Such analytics often provide insights that can inform promotional campaigns, including predicting which promotions will generate desired sales brand further into the future, marketing executives need use judgment, combining analytics with their own and others' insight and experience.

The application of experience and expertise to critical business decisions and practice represents the real value of human judgment. But, when artificial intelligent machines are implemented to any organizations to assist the low, middle and top level management to make any business judgment. These forms of judgment work that managers can gather data interpretation, idea development more absolute from (AI) machine assistance. Thus, why these level management executives need to learn how to apply (AI) machines to help them to make any business judgment more accurate.

● How (AI) influences organizational change

Consequently creative and social intelligence will be in even greater demand as (AI) makes in management and the workforce. This development will represent a long term trend in labor markets , one characterized by intensifying demand and reward for social skills with a growing desire for creative capabilities, managers will seek to fashion of ideas and hypotheses from inside and outside of the enterprise to shape solutions to their most pressing business problems. Thus, (AI) will influence overall organizational team members who have chance to participate any decision to make more accurate business judgment.

Many managers mistakenly view judgment work as only an individual discipline, failing to appreciate that it can also involve decide interpersonal and organizational practices. In more complex settings, judgment is typically a collective outcome of individuals' and teams' diverse perspectives, insights and experiences. And often , the resulting choices are better informed than decisions that an individual would have arrived at on his or her own.

Thus, when any organizations apply (AI) technology to assist managers to gather data and ideas to make any judgment. In these cases, organizations can create the conditions for effective collective judgment by establishing structures , such as " shadow advisory boards" that prompt managers and employees to source and synthesize multiple perspectives. Thus, a traditional organization (firm) might freshen its thinking is t put together a shadow advisory board, comprised of young, digital people who can apply (AI) machine assistance to make judgment work more accurate whether related to people development, problem-solving or strategizing and innovating for considerable degrees of creative and social intelligence.

Thus, on the one hand, (AI) technology machine augmentation and automation can give these advantages to human (organization managers) , e.g. developing people and community, solving problems and collaborating, coordinating and controlling work, shaping strategy and leading innovation. Besides, on the other hand, the next generation managers need have these individual attitude to treat intelligent machines to be as colleagues.

When, judgment is a human skill, intelligent machines can accelerate human learning that supports it, assisting in data -driven simulations, scenarios and search and discovery activities. Focuses on judgment work, some decisions require insight beyond what data can tell them. This is the sweet sport for human judgment, the application of experience and expertise to critical business decisions and practices. Thus, managers will also need to find ways to learn how to use digital (AI) technologies to tap into the knowledge and judgment of partners, customer external stakeholders and role models in other industries after the (AI) machine had been implemented to the organization.

5.3 Future works change: Automation, employment and productivity
● How (AI) influences employment
Human future " micro to macro" industry trends will be affected business strategy and public policy by (AI) technology. In the future (AI) technology will influence those six themes: productivity and growth, natural resources, labor markets, the evolution of global financial markets, the economic impact of technology and innovation and urbanization. However, (AI) technology will bring economic benefits of tackling gender inequality, a new global competition, Chinese innovation and digital globalization.
Nowadays, advances in robotics artificial intelligence, and machine learning are in a new age of automation, as machines match or outperform human performance in a development to any countries. For example, automation of activities can enable businesses to improve performance by reducing errors and improving quality and speed, and in some cases achieving outcomes that go beyond human capabilities. For example, some research indicated automation could raise productivity growth globally by 0.8 to 1.4 % annually; more than 2,000 work activities across 800 occupations. When less than 5% of all occupations can be automated using demonstrated technologies about 60% of all occupations have at least 30% of constituent activities that could be automated. Many occupations will change that will be automated away: Activities most susceptible to automation involve physical activities, in highly structured and predictable environments, as well as the collection and processing of data. They are most prevalent in manufacturing , accommodation and food service and retail trade and include some middle-skill jobs. For example, such as natural language processing is a key factor. Beyond technical feasibility, the cost of technology competition with labor including skills and supply and demand

dynamics, performance benefits including and beyond labor cost savings, and social and regulatory acceptance will be affected by (AI) automation technology. Thus, (AI) automation will impact to influence global employment in those aspects as below:

Firstly, assuming that people are displaced by automation will find other employment. The anticipated shift in the activities in the labor force is of a similar order as the long-term shift away from agriculture and decreases in manufacturing share of employment. Both of manufacturing and agriculture industries which would be accompanied by the creation of new types of work not foreseen at the time.

Secondly, for business, the performance benefits of automation are relatively clear. Thus, the businessmen have opportunities for their micro economies to benefits from the productivity growth potential and macro economies to benefit to encourage continued progress and innovation , investment and market incentives. At the same time, employers must innovate policies to help workers and institutions adapt to the impact on employment.

This will likely include rethinking education and training, income support and safety nets , as well as support for those dislocated, when employees need to leave themselves homes to move to other cities to learn new (AI) automation works. Thus, individuals in the workplace will need to engage move comprehensively with machines as part of their everyday activities, and acquire new skills that will be in demand in the new automation age. Consequently , the scale of shifts in the labor force over many decades that automation technologies can be a similar order to the long -term technology -enables shifts in the developed countries' workforces away from agriculture in the 21 th century. Those shifts did not result in long-term mass unemployment because they were accompanied by the creation of new types of work not foreseen at the time. However, human will still be needed in the workforce when the total productivity gains are caused by (AI) technology.

● What occupations will be influenced by (AI) technology.

In the future, scientists predict that these occupations will be influenced by (AI) technology mostly. They include : retail salespeople, food and beverage service workers, language or translation teachers, health practitioners. Since these work activities have a more relevant occupations are made up of a range of activities with different potential for (AI) automation . For example, a retail salesperson will spend more time interacting with customers, stocking shelves , or ringing up sales. Each of these activities is distinct and requires different capabilities to perform successfully.

Thus, these job activities have similar simple control characteristics. Simple activities include greet customers, answer questions about products and services, clean and maintain work areas, demonstrate product feature process sales and transactions. All these activities can have similar simple activities in order to (AI) machines can be learn how to do these activities from (AI) technology . For example, the capability perception includes sensory perception, cognitive capabilities, such as retrieving automation, recognizing known patterns(supervised learning), logical reasoning problem solving.

Thus, (AI) machine is such human, which has feeling and emotion, such as social and emotional sensing, judgement reasoning methods, natural language understanding and physical capabilities, such as mobility , navigation, gross motor skill, fine motor skills. It seems that the future, (AI) human invents machines which will have these human characteristics to do human similar behavioral job duties more easily and efficiently. It implies these above human occupations will be replaced by (AI) human invention machines in the future. Due to (AI) creation, it is possible to cause unemployment number of these above workers will increase because (AI) machines can do their similar job behavioral activities.

Consequently, employers won't need to employ many of these skillful labor. Otherwise, they can buy less number (AI) machines to attempt to do whose job activities more easily and efficiently. So, it seems (AI) machines will have more high work performance to replace these occupation workers' work performance. Finally, these occupation worker unemployment number will only increase when the (AI) machines had been invented to achieve to do their work behavioral activities absolutely success in the future.

● Whether (A) technology machine labor
will replace human worker more or assist
human worker more

There is no single agreed definition of a robot how outcome of a task that is completed without human intervention. When some definitions require the task to be completed by a physical machine moves and respond to its environment, other definitions use the term robot in connection with tasks completed by software , without physical embodiment.

However, to answer the question : Whether (AI) technology machine labor will replace human worker more or assist human worker more. I shall indicate some examples to let readers to judge whether (AI) technology can create new jobs or reduce old jobs.

Firstly, I shall explain what (AI) function is. (AI) is a service robot that performs useful tasks for humans or equipment excluding industrial automation application . Thus, the classification of a robot into industrial robot or service robot is done according to its intended application. It is also a personal service robot or a service robot for personal used for a non commercial task, usually by lay persons . Examples are domestic servant robot, and pet exercising robot. It is also a professional service robot or a service robot for professional used for a commercial task, usually operated by a properly trained operator. Examples, are cleaning robot for public places, delivery robot in offices or hospitals, fire-fighting robot, rehabilitation robot and surgery robot in hospitals. Thus, these functions will be future (AI) application to our daily life necessaries or business necessaries.

However, some authors agree (AI) will bring negative outcomes of automation, due to raise competiveness, reduce human job nature. Otherwise, other authors argue (AI) will bring positive outcomes of automation, due to raise productivities, job creation, assist humans work.

On the positive outcome hand, robots can increase productivity . This is particularly important for small-to medium sized businesses both are in developed and developing countries economies. It also enables large companies to increase their competitiveness through faster product development and delivery. Increased use of robot is also enabling companies in high cost countries to re shore, or bring back to their domestic base parts of the supply chain that will have previously outsourced to sources of cheaper labor. Currently , the greater threat to employment is not a automation, but an inability to remain competitive. Automation has led overall to an increase in labor demand and positive impact on wages. The reason is that the middle-income/middle-skilled jobs have reduced as a proportion of overall contribution to employment and earnings leading to fears of increasing income inequality, the skills range within the middle income bracket is large. Thus, robots are driving an increase in demand for workers at the higher -skilled and with a positive impact on wages. This issue is how to enable middle-income earners in the lower-income range to unskilled or retain. Finally, the (AI) positive impact supporter who argue the future will be robots and humans can work together.

However, on the negative outcome hand, robots can substitute labor activities, but don't replace jobs. They believe that less than 10% of jobs are fully automatable. Increasingly , robots are used to complement and augment labor activities, the net impact on jobs and the quality of work is positive. Automation can provide the opportunity for humans to focus on higher-skilled, higher-quality and higher-paid tasks. Robots can improve productivity when they are applied to tasks that which perform more efficiently and to a higher and more consistent level of quality than humans. For example, increased productivity is enabling some firms, such as Whirlpool, Caterpillar and Ford Motors company in the US restructure their supply chains, bringing back parts of the manufacturing process to the country of origin. Thus, productivity gains due to robotics and automation are important not just at the company level, but also for build industry and nation competitiveness.

I suppose that productivity can be raised. What are the impacts of robots on employment? Firstly, the main focus of development has been on personal entertainment, which does not drive worker productivity (manufacturing production). When the internet (information and communication technology (ICT)) innovation. This is borne and by findings that manufacturing productivity, which has been driven by innovations in automation rather than consumer technologies, has government strongly than productivity in the services sectors of the economy in most nature economies. It seems (AI) automation will create many jobs in internet communication entertainment game industry. For example, many young people like to use internet to play any electronic games from computer or mobile at home or outside home conveniently. Thus, (AI) automation will increase demand to be invented to any new entertainment game from internet channel. It will need to employ many (AI) entertainment game inventors to create many automation entertainment games. Thus, (AI) automation in internet entertainment game industry will need human (AI) entertainment game inventors to invent the knowledge-based capital of (AI) automation entertainment games. The (AI) entertainment game inventors will need own research and development skills, form specific skills, organizational know-how skills, databased knowledge, design and various forms of intellectual property to do these (AI) automation entertainment game invention occupations in the future.

International Federation Of Robotics(2016) indicated that China will be as a major robotics manufacturer and user of robots, benefiting from jobs created by robot manufacturing and productivity gains from robot use. Chins had sold of robots to any one single market every year since 2017 year. The Chinese government has included a focus on robotics in its 10 year strategy. In order to achieve its target of a robot density of 150 units per 10, 000 workers by 2020 year. Thus, Chinese companies will have to install around 650,000 new industrial robots between 2016 to 2020 year, 2.5 times more than installed globally in 2015 year.

Hence, China (AI) manufacturing industry will need to employ many workers . It implies (AI) manufacturing industry will create many new occupations in China. Also, ministry of economy, trade and industry (2015) also showed that Japan currently has the largest stock of industrial robots in operations, primarily in the automation industry. Driven by a rapidly aging population and low productivity rates, the Japanese government has sights on a 20-fold increase in the use of robots in the non-manufacturing sector and a three-fold growth rate of labor productivity in the service sector both by 2020 year. Thus, it also implies Japan will need many robots to be provide to service industry. Due to robots will provide to serve any businessmen's clients. Thus, it is possible that the service workers won't be dismissed as well as it is depended on the serving job nature to decide whether Japan's service workers can still serve to their employer when the service (AI) robots are applied to whose employers.

Consequently, it seems that (AI) can create employment, Ministry of economy, trade and industry (2015) showed that such as China will develop the major (AI) automation manufacturing industry. The (AI) employers will need to employ many workers to manufacture any these different kinds of (AI) robots to satisfy China or overseas individual or business buyers needs. But, (AI) can also cause unemployment to the low skillful service workers. Such as if Japan some service businesses choose to buy any (AI) service robots to replace their service staffs to serve their clients. It is possible that the service staffs will be dismissed, due to (AI) robots can do such as their same service job duties to achieve better service performance.

Thus, today, it is increasingly common for people to use robots in various situations at home and in retail stores, hotels and hospitals these service industries. Robots are classified into server types based on their functionality (service and utility robots or those designed to communicate with humans) and appearance (humanoid robots or mechanical robots). The type of robot, to which each country allocated particular importance in the advance of robotics, reflects the sense of values and preferences of its population. Thus, if the country has high population needs to use robots, then they will influence either more new jobs creation or more old job loss in the country's (AI) manufacturing or (AI) service industries both. For example, Japan respondents often associate the term " robot " with humanoid robots that can communicate with human and they have a high level of familiarity with robot. The US has the highest level of robot utilization at home and in retail stores with its people being the most enthusiastic about the future use of robots. Germany shows a strong tendency to consider robots for industrial purposes and its people feel strong effort to the presence of robots in their households.

In conclusion, to judge whether how (AI) will influence the country's employment to be better or worse. It will depend on the country home buyers (users) or business buyers (users) how to use (AI) for their daily needs. If the country , such as US retail stores need to use (AI) , it will have possible to reduce some or many retail service workers. Even, if the country , such as Japan has many home users need to use (AI) , it will not influence the employment market. Otherwise, it will raise (AI) salespeople numbers. Even, if the country, such as Germany and China will have many (AI) manufacturers, then it will create many (AI) manufacturing occupations for these (AI) manufactory workers.

Consequently, (AI) robots manufacturing and service needs will have positive or negative impact to any country's employment. It will depend on the (AI) service provision and service workers' job nature as well as the manufacturing workers of (AI) knowledge level to decide their employment chance in their country's employment market.

5.4 How can (AI) influence labor market?
● How can human society job nature
to be changed to artificial intelligent society?

From the first intelligent perspective reason view point, artificial intelligence is making machines " intelligent" acting as humans expect people to act. Artificial intelligence has ability to distinguish computer responses from human responses, it owns knowledge to solve expert problem. From another research perspective reason view point, artificial intelligence is the study of how to make computers do things which, at the moment, people do better (Rich & Knight, 1991, p.3).

(AI) researchers are native in a variety of domains, e.g. formal tasks (mathematics, games), tasks (perception, robotics, natural language, common sense reasoning), expert tasks (financial analysis, medical diagnostics, engineering, scientific analysis and other areas).

From the second business perspective reason view point, (AI) is a set of many powerful tools, and methodologies for using those tools to solve business problems. From a programming perspective reason view point, (AI) includes the study of symbolic programming problem solving and search .

From the third human technological perspective reason view point, today's computer can do many well-defined tasks, for example, arithmetic operations, are much faster and more accurate than human beings. However, the computers' interaction with their environment is not very sophisticated yet. How can human test whether a computer has reached the general intelligence level of a human being? Can a computer convince a human interrogator that it is a human? But before thinking of such advanced kinds of machines, human will start developing our own extremely simple " intelligent" machines.

So, it is possible that human society job nature will to be changed to artificial intelligent society when (AI) technology is developed to the mature stage in the future.

● Why does human need artificial intelligence machines?

One of major division in (AI) is between humans who think (AI) is the only serious way of finding out how we (human) work and human who want companies to do very smart things, independently of how we (human) work. This is the important distinction between cognitive scientists vs engineers. One of another major division in (AI) is between symbolic (AI), which represents information through symbols and their relationships. Specific Algorithms are used to process these symbols to solve problems or deduce new knowledge and connectionist. So (AI) , which represents information in network. Biological processes underlying learning, task performance and problem solving are imitated from human mind behaviors.

Thus, it is possible that artificial intelligence machines can do the better judgicious behavior to compare human.

● How does artificial intelligence influence future working changing in automation employment and productivity aspects?

In the automation changing influence aspect, as companies increasingly use robots on production lines or algorithms to optimize their logistics manage inventory, any carry out other core business functions. Technological advances are creating a new automation age in which ever-smarter and more flexible machines will be deployed on an ever larger scale in the marketplace. However, researching artificial intelligence with how influences human working nature. We need to answer these questions: How will automation transform the workplace? What will the implications for employment? And what is likely to be its impact both on productivity in the global economy and on employment?

Advances in robotics, artificial intelligence, and machine learning are growing in a new age of automation as machines match or outperform human performance in a range of work activities, including ones requiring cognitive capabilities. What factors are determined the changing in workplace adoption by artificial intelligence innovation? What advantages are automation? Automation of activities can be enabled businesses to improve performance by reducing errors and improving quality and speed, and achieving outcomes that go beyond human capabilities.

Some scientists indicated based on their scenario modeling. They estimated automation could raise producing growth globally by 0.8 to 1.4 percent annually. Almost, the activities people are paid almost $16 trillion in wages to do in global economy have the potential to be automated by adopting currently demonstrated technology. According to their analysis of more than 2,000 work activities across 800 occupations. When less than 5% of all occupations have of least 30% of activities that could be automated. They also indicated that technical economic and social factors will determine automation. Continued technical progress, for example, in areas such as natural language processing is a key factor beyond technical feasibility , the cost of technology, competition with labor including skills, and supply and demand dynamics, performance benefits including and beyond labor cost savings and social and regulatory acceptance will affect (alter) the scope of automation.

Other some scientists also indicate U.S. country for example, the anticipate shift in the activities in labor force of a similar order of magnitude as the long term sight away from agriculture and decreases in manufacturing. Share of employment in the United States both which were achieved. So, those factors can influence why artificial intelligence technology needs. So, it is possible that future agriculture and manufacturing both industries will apply (AI) technology manufacturer-kind of job nature to raise productivity instead of farmers, fruit picking workers, farming transportation labours as well as factory manufacturing workers and supervisors etc. human-kind of job nature.

● Is artificial intelligence possible to replace labor ?

Not just intelligence, but also debating, if machines are capable of having a conscious minds. Artificial intelligence has those characteristics as below:

On functionalism aspect, artificial intelligence inputs mental states, sensory inputs, (beliefs, desires being in pain feeling) and behavioral outputs. Since mental states are identified by a functional role, which are thoughts to be manifested in various systems. Even, perhaps computers which are physical devices with electronic substrate that inform computations on inputs to give outputs similar to brains which are artificial intelligence composed of part any intrinsic relationship to each other. Thus, artificial intelligence activities is not the whole itself, but into parts or on external influence on the parts.

On dualism aspect, artificial intelligence is a set of views about the relationship between mind are matter. On materialism aspect, it builds the only thing that exists is matter, including consciousness.

On biological naturalism aspect, it is similar a human brain than feels pains makes mental situation. So, artificial intelligence is similar biologist which might to be excited to human labor work. Hence, it seems artificial intelligence can change (alter) or replace human labor work of nature in possible in the future.

● Can (AI) technology replace human labour nature of work?

On technological innovation reason view point, the history development of artificial intelligence studying the intelligence is one of most ancient scientific discipline. The history development of artificial intelligence what aims to achieve human use to sense, learn remember and think, logic probability, decision making and calculation develop from mathematics, instead of replacement human labor functions.

Artificial intelligence history development aim is the scientific analysis of skills in connection and practice with the appearance of computers from 1950 year beginning. The artificial intelligence (AI) can deal with the ultimate challenges. How can (either biological or electronic) mind sense, understand and manipulate a world that is much simple and more complex than itself? And what if would human like to construct something with such capabilities?

The general-purpose software of the early period of (AI) were only able to solve simple tasks effectively and failed when which should be used in a wider range or an more difficult tasks. One of the sources of difficulty was that early software had very few or mix knowledge about the problems which handled, and activities successes by simply syntactic manipulation. Moreover, the other difficulty was that many problems that were tried to solve by the (AI) were untreatable.

The early (AI) software whether trying step sequences based on the basic facts about the problem that should be solved, experimented with different combinations till which found a solution. From the end the 1960 year, developing the so-called expert systems were emphasized. These systems had (sue-based) knowledge base about the field which handled. Till to the beginning of the 1970 year, (Prolog) the logical programming language was born, which was built in the computation realization of a version of the resolution calculus. (Prolog) is a remarkably prevalent tool in developing expert systems (on medical, judiciary and other scopes), but natural language parsers were implemented in this language. Then, in 1981 s, the Japanese announced the fifth generation computer system project, a 10 years plan to build an intelligent computer system that use the (Prolog) language as a machine code. Nowadays, (AI) can be applied any industries, such as car manufacturing industry can use (AI) technological machine-men manufacture car, instead of replacing human labors in factory. Even, in the future, using (AI) machine-men drivers can drive any private cars or public transportation tools, instead of replacing human drivers, e.g. bus, train, tram, ferry etc. Also in the future, machine-men can replace housewives to serve families to do housekeeping clean job , e.g. cleaning toilets, bathrooms, kitchens, even cooking functions at home. So (AI) machine-man can reduce housewives works at home. Moreover, (AI) machine man can take care old people , when who are living at homes or elder care centers.

So, it seems artificial intelligence (AI) will be possible developed to manufacture a new generation machine-man to assist (serve) families to do any simply cleaning or cooking jobs at homes. Moreover, the overall demand of (AI) general social needs will also rise, such as security, driving transportation tools, restaurant cleaning, elder centers care service etc. So, it seems that individual or families or social needs of (AI) will be increase in the future. Thus, it will influence macro economy growth (GDP) if there are large house family consumer group and hotel or bus or taxis or ferry etc. different business consumer group demand any artificial intelligence machine numbers increasing. Then, the artificial intelligence products and material manufacturers must need to buy many artificaial intelligence materials to produce any kinds of artificial intelligence machines to prepare to satisfy consumer individual needs. Consequently, macro economy will grow to the owned artificial intelligence development countries, e.g. US, China, UK.

● Why can artificial intelligence satisfy human needs?

First, On machine-man satisfactory demand aspect view point, it makes computers that think, it is the automation of activities. We associate with human thinking: like decision making, learning. It is the act of creating machine that perform function that require intelligence when performed by people. It is the study of mental faculties through the use of computational models. It is the study of computations that make it possible to perceive, reason and act. It is a branch of computer science that is concerned with the automation of intelligent behavior. It is anything in computing service that human don't yet know how to do property.

Second, on thought aspect artificial intelligence means systems thank think like humans, systems that think rationally.

Third, on behavioral aspect, artificial intelligence systems that act like human and that systems act rationally. However, the basic objective of (AI) is to represent human's thought processes in computation . These machines are supposed to exhibit behavior that. It is performed by a human being, would be considered intelligent. However, some authors feel (AI) has disadvantages, such as it is not creative, it is excited in the use of sensory devices, it can't make use of a very wide context of experiences and it does not use common sense.

For speech recognition and understanding function needs example, (AI) can be applied in speech recognition and understanding function, which (AI) speech or voice recognition is a data input method. For example, the computer recognizes and understands one (or a few) word commands. Speech understanding on the other hand is the computer's ability to understanding a spoken language. That is , the computer understands the meaning of sentences, an paragraphs through (AI).

So, (AI) can be attempted to learn human language how to speak. It is similar to translate human language skill, instead of actual human speaking skill. Also, (AI) can assist handicap learning or language student how to listen different languages by machine-man sounds from computers more accurately. So, it seems that it (AI) can replace human language teachers speaking function and can change teaching language nature of job in language speaking and listening education industry.

● Is artificial intelligence one good choice for human future technological benefit?

Nowadays, new technology development is popular. However, artificial intelligence is one kind of new technology choice among different technologies innovation. So it brings this question: Is artificial intelligence technology value to invest? To answer this question. I shall indicate some other new technology developments to compare (AI) technology development to judge which has urgent needs to achieve human expectation nowadays.

For example, why is green peace interested in new technologies? New technologies features prominently in our ongoing campaigns against genetic modified crops and number power. However, which are also an integral part of our solutions to environmental challenges, including renewable energy technologies, such as solar, wind and wave (water) power energy as well as waste treatment technologies, such as mechanical, biological treatment. It seems humans need concern how to apply (AI) technology to solve environment pollution challenges in our future. So, environment protective, agriculture, natural energy technology will be popular demand to attempt to apply (AI) technology to solve their challenges or apply (AI) to assist to develop their industry.

● How can artificial intelligence impact on workplace?

Modern information technologies and the labor economy growth of machines is powered by artificial intelligence have already strongly influenced the world of work in the 21 ST century. Computers, algorithms and software simplify every tasks and it is impossible to image how most of our life could be managed without them. How can be the information economy characterized by exponential growth replaces the most production industry based on economy of scales? What will the future world of work look like and how long will it take to get? Will the future world of work be a world where humans spend less time earning their livelihood? Alternatively, are mass unemployment, mass poverty and social distortions also possible scenario for the future, where robots, artificial intelligence systems play an increasingly central role? These questions concern how artificial intelligence further development . Can influence labor economy growth on workplace ? When the labor market has widespread impact on intelligence property, information technology, product liability, competition and labor and employment laws.

How (AI) technology impacts on labor workplace.

The future influence any organizations how labor economies use of (AI) can be analyzed, such as deep machine learning is based on a set of model high level data. Unlike human workers, the machines are connected the whole time in workplace. If one machine makes a mistake, all autonomous systems will keep this in mind and will avoid the same mistake the next time.

Over the long run intelligent machines will win against every human expert. Production robots have been replacing employees because of the (AI) technology. They work more precisely than humans and cost loss. Creative solutions like 3D printers and the self learning ability of these production robots will replace human workers, the automatic data recording and data processing, traditional back office activities are no longer in demand. Autonomous software will collect necessary information and will send it to the employee who needs it. Additionally, dematerialization leads to the phenomenon that traditional physical products are becoming software. For example, CD or DVDs are being replaced by streaming services. The replacement of traditional event ticket, e-travel ticket service products or hard cash will be the next step, due to the possibility of payment by smartphone. So, (AI) technology will impact human's daily life consumption behaviors in the future. For another example, transportation tools, such as boats and ferries and private vehicles will use sensors and navigating without human input. Taxi and truck drivers will become obsolete, the stock store applies to stock managers and postal carriers of the delivery is distributed by (AI) machine delivery method.

What is the relationship between (AI) and (CRM)?

● Can (AI) technology impact on customer relationship management (CRM) ?

Nowadays , (AI) is a technology almost as old as the computer industry itself, it is similar with the advent of personal assistants function to businesses and personal promotion channel, such as (Amazon's Alexa, Apple's Siri, Google's Assistant) image recognition (face book), personalized recommendations (Netflix , Amazon). Those innovations have been driven by a increase in processing power, lower cost hardware, and the exploding creation and availability of data. It seems, (AI) technology can impact global customer service management method.

How to forecast economic impact modeling to (AI) will affect global economy? Can human forecast business revenue growth and job creation (or destruction) based on (AI) applied to customer relationship management (CRM) activities? In addition to the economic impact on (AI) or (CRM) which can include an estimate of the economic impact attributable to sales forces customer base. What can economic benefits be brought to (CRM) from (AI) technology?

Artificial intelligence(AI) comprises a set of technologies that use natural language processing, machine learning, knowledge graphs, and other tools to answer questions, discover insights and provide recommendations. Computer systems can use (AI) hypothesize and formulate possible answers based on available evidence can be trained through the ingestion of vast amounts of content, and automatically adapt and learn from (AI) self mistakes and failures.

So, any business organizations (customer service departments) can provide efficient and effective customer relationship management of excellent customer service quality if which applied (AI) technology system. The different type of (AI) systems include: (AI) system platforms, machine learning (AI) based data preparation and enrichment tools, machine vision/ image recognition, voice speech recognition, text analysis and natural language processing, bots , e.g. face book website and virtual digital assistance solutions, social media pattern analysis , sentiment analysis, advanced numerical analysis (e.g. IOT streaming , machine logs), supporting technologies, knowledge base dialog management, Q&A processing etc. different (AI) technology system customer relationship management (CRM) tools.

(AI) (CRM) of activity can include these categories, such as: corporate marketing, marketing operation, field marketing, customer support, digital commerce, customer analytics, customer influenced product or service design, product or service pricing, finance information, presentation, customer billing, inventory , logistics and fulfilment support, partner management etc. different CRM tools.

(AI) technology of CRM has been carrying on plan different stages to achieve CRM personal assistant tool for businesses. The stages are such as, in the beginning stage of (AI) projects in place, implement now, pilot phase next year in the final stage of (AI) customer relationship management tools are foreseeable future. So, this CRM technology has been improved to plan in different stages every year to prepare to achieve full capacity of CRM service quality for businesses to use in the future.

Hence, how to develop an estimate prediction of the economic impact (AI) technologies could have CRM activities, which depends on gathering macroeconomic information on business revenue and the basic marketing of business revenue and the basic markup of business expenses by major functions (customer support, marketing and sales , production etc.)

An economic impact model that can gather data together and forecast the results how (AI) artificial intelligence technology brings (CRM) customer relationship management benefits to businesses, e.g. surveys investigation includes IT spending by sample countries, GDP and population estimates and forecasts, revenue per employee and ratios of IT spend to GDP. Surveys (questionnaire questions) of forecast results are influenced by (AI) impact can include: results are projected from surveys and rely on estimates are made by respondents on the expected financial improvements in categories of (AI) –assisted customer relationship management activities. The forecast assumes that these estimates are correct; financial estimates are based on estimates of "first year" improvement from full (AI) implementation; forecasts are from planning to implement any artificial intelligence of customer relationship management (CRM) projects, the improvement forecast is of categories of activity , e.g. corporate marketing , digital commerce, and customer analytics. They are not estimates of ROI for the (AI) software. They rely on conservative estimates to which each of these entities might affect company revenue, expenses or productivity. They also rely on estimates of the penetration of software in customer relationship management activities . Net new jobs created are based on the ratio of new revenue to jobs required to support that revenue . They can assume that 50% of the net new revenue will support increases in labor and the rest will go for capital and other operating expenses that may replace jobs lost to automation.

In the future, some of the ways in micro economic benefits to any organizations. (AI) technology is expected to impact CRM activities include: Spending up sales cycles, improving lead generation and qualification solving customer support problems faster (raising service quality), helping companies improve brand campaigns and recognition, lowering costs of support calls when increasing resolution rates, lowering the cost of recruiting employees and partners, increasing revenue from optimized product marketing, optimizing price, distribution logistics and preventing loss through fraud detection. So, micro economic benefits view point, it seems that (AI) CRM technology can raise any companies economic benefits for care term.

Artificial intelligence enables machines or the in-build software to behave like human beings which allows these decisions and act. The advent of (AI) is leading , talking, making decisions and act. The advent of (AI) is leading to new technologies advances and transforming the economic and employment opportunities for humans in a positive way. (AI) related technologies can facilitate our live. For example, industrial robotics, robotic medical assistants, smart games, financial forecasting software, big data analysis, algorithms in health and bioinformatics, pilotless cargo places, drone ambulances and general purpose and workplace robots and others. (Disruptors technologies: Advances that will transform life, business and the global economy).

Artificial intelligence also known as computational intelligence is defined as " the human –like intelligence exhibited by machines or software. It is theorized that intelligence of humans can be described and intelligence machines or software can simulate it. These machines software can be reasonable , learn, perceive and process information, like human mind and thus facilitate human life. They can think and act for us. So, artificial intelligence is an interdisciplinary field of study including computer science, neuroscience, psychology, linguistics and philosophy.

However, (AI) research and developments have economically impacted many industries, such as robotics, telecommunications, computer applications , health, finance, heavy manufacturing, transportation, aviation, e-service and e-commerce, military , music and movie, toys and games entertainment etc. industries.

In fact, many ideas, systems and technologies have been developing in the world of (AI) technology. However, which are net called or considered (AI) products, rather which are mentioned with their specific names, such as smart graphics, machine learning, e-commerce etc. (i.e. this is called (AI) effect).

● How does (AI) technology influence
the future of employment change?

Are future nature of jobs changed to computerization from (AI) technology? Where are the probability of computing occupations from (AI) technology influence? What is expected impacts of future computing on labor market from (AI) technology influence? John Maynard Keynes's frequently cited prediction of widespread technological unemployment " du to our discovery of means of economic the use of labor outrunning the pace of which we can find new used of labor" (Keynes, 1933, p.3).

In the future, (AI) technology will impact some nature of occupations to change computing. This chance will also influence some countries' economic change. For example, some factory human labors hand routine manufacturing tasks will be changed to computerization of routine manufacturing tasks by (AI) technological machine men hand manufacturing method. it will cause a structured shift in the labor market, with workers reallocating their labor supply from middle-income manufacturing to low-income service occupations.

Arguably, this is because the manual tasks of service occupations are less computerization, as who require a higher degree of flexibility and physical adaptability. So, (AI) technology will influence the human hand labor skillful occupation nature of task cheaper , such as vehicle manufacturing , ship manufacturing, computer manufacturing, steel manufacturing, television, radio etc. home electronic products of heavy machine industry change. Due to (AI) technology machine man will be proper to be used to manufacturing these electronic products when the (AI) technology innovation can develop to the mature stage. Then, any countries manufacturers will choose to use (AI) technology machine man, instead of human hand production.

Supposing the future prices of computing are fallen, seriously, problem solving skills are becoming relatively productive, explaining the substantial employment growth in manufacturing occupations, involving cognitive tasks where skilled labor has a comparative advantage, as well as the increase education needs for (AI) technology computing of machine man subject study.

Prediction of education needs for (AI) technology student numbers will increase, due to manufacturing industry needs many (AI) technology students in future employment market. Another (AI) technology influence if the future (AI) technological innovation, e.g. machine man manufacturing or machine man service industries will both increase demand, then with more sophistic software technologies will be disrupted labor markets by marketing workers redundant.

For publishing industry, what is striking about the case in paper book publishing industry will be unpopular? Due to the electronic book publishing industry will be popular, e.g. Amazon publish . (AI) technology can influence paper book manufacturing method which is replaced by machine man electronic book manufacturing method as well as it will cause the computerization is no longer confined to routine manufacturing tasks. Due to (AI) machine man manufacturing technology will be proper to be used to manufacture any products in short time efficiently and effectively , e.g. electronic book products. In the future, if it is fact to occur this case, such as (AI) technological machine man manufacturing method will be adopted (applied) to manufacture electronic books or any products in possible. (AI) technology will cause many manufacturing workers are unemployed. It is beneficial to employers, who can reduce to spend much wages expenditure to employ manufacturing workers, but it will cause many manufacturing workers loss jobs and reduce income to support whose families lives. It will cause social challenges, e.g. increasing stealing crimes if the manufacturing workers had not other skills to find other jobs to do easily. So, manufacturers need to concern over technological unemployment which will be hardly future phenomenon if who decided to dismiss all manufacturing workers, due to (AI) technology machine men replace to them.

If (AI) technology can be innovated to produce any kinds of machine man to serve any service or manufacturing industries successfully. Then, it will bring these questions: Can future that workers be influenced to be automation employment and productivity by (AI) technology influence? Does it impact to influence the (AI) technology countries' productivity and growth and natural resources development and labor markets and evolution of global financial markets and economic impact of technology and innovation and urbanization etc. issues? How will automation transform the workplace? What will be the implication for employment? What is likely to be its impact both on productivity in the global economy and on employment?

In fact, automatic of activities can enable businesses to improve performance by reducing errors chance and improving quality and speed, and same cases achieving outcomes that go beyond human capabilities. Some economists indicate (AI) technology would give a needed boost to economic growth and prosperity have of the working age population in many countries. Based on the scenario modeling, they estimate automation could raise productivity growth globally by 0.8 to 1.4 % annually. They also indicated that almost half the activities people are almost $1.6 trillion in wages to do in the global economy have the potential to be automated adapting current demonstrates technology, according to their analysis of more than 2,000 work activities across 800 occupations. When less than 5% of all occupations can be automated entirely using demonstrated technology, about 60% of all occupations have at least 30% of worker made activities, that would be automated. More occupation will change to be automated. They also indicated for business performance benefits of automation are relatively clear, but the issues are more complicated by policy making to attract foreign investors. Beyond technical feasibility, the cost of technology, competition labor will include skills and supply and demand dynamics, performance benefits and beyond labor cost savings and social and regulatory acceptance will affect the automation. Their predictions suggest that half of today work activities could be automated by 2055 year, but this could happen 10 to 20 years earlier or latter depending on the various factors in addition to their wider economic condition.

Some scientists suggest (AI) technology is finally starting to deliver real-life business benefits. Computer power is growing significantly , algorithms are becoming more sophisticated and perhaps most important of all, the world is generating vast quantities of the fuel that powers (AI) technology data billions of gigabytes of it every day. Also, online firms are digital natives, such as Google online search service company is investing on (AI) technology. For new though most of the news if coming from the suppliers of (AI) technologies. And many new users are only in the experimental phase. Few products are on the market or are likely to arrive these soon to drive immediate and widespread adoption. As a result, analysts believe (AI) technology's potential will give true economic benefit in the future. (AI) industry will introduce to suppliers and users to raise economic potential of (AI) technology.

In the future, (AI) technology systems can solve business problems. Some scientists categorized those into five technology systems that are key areas of (AI) technology development: robotics and autonomous vehicles, computer vision language virtual agents and machine learning , which is based on algorithms that learn from data without replying on rules-based programming in order to draw conclusions or direct an action.

Such as computer vision and language includes natural language processing, analytics, speech recognition technology, some are about learning from information, such as about machine learning and others are related to acting on information, such as robotics, autonomous vehicles and virtual agents, which are computer programs that can converse with humans. Machine learning and a subfield called deep learning are artificial intelligence applications.

● Can artificial intelligence impact

global office productive efficiency ?

Artificial intelligence (AI) is a term first defined in 1956 year. It is a branch of computer science that aims to create intelligent machines that work and react like humans. In contrast today, 60 years later, (AI) is characterized by a number of applications, including computers playing games against humans and understanding human languages, virtual personal assistants, and robotics which involve computers seeing , hearing and reacting to sensory stimuli. In the future, technologists predict for (AI) technology ranging from (AI) being used as a tool to aid relatively simple processes for robots with human like mental capabilities, who expect (AI) technology can emulate human performance by learning, coming to mind its own conclusions, understanding complex content, engaging in dialog with people, enhancing human cognitive performance or replacing humans in executing both routine and non-routine tasks. In existing industry, (AI) technology is used , such as targeted advertising and virtual used personal assistant as well as the (AI) technology that my exist in the future, such as robots with human vehicle processing capabilities.

The range of (AI) technology's progress in the future will determine the economic impact future of (AI) technology on the global economy with more limited advances and applications (i.e. weak (AI) only) corresponding to more limited economic impacts and more substantial progress, i.e. strong (AI) technology is corresponding to more significant economic impact.

(AI) technology learning that automates analytical model, including predicting

cause-and-effect relationship from biological data, identifying new drugs, self-driving cars and protecting against fraud etc. functions. Also (AI) learning can improve natural language processing that allows computers to continue to better analyze, understand and generate language to interface with human using the natural human language, virtual personal assistant, helps users by providing scheduling appointment, reminds organizing personal finance and finding providers of various services, machine vision allows (AI) machine man to identify object, scenes and activities in detect pedestrians and bicyclists.

We expect the economic effects of (AI) technology to include both direct GDP growth from sectors that develop or manufacture (AI) technology and indirect GDP growth through increased productivity in existing sectors that employ some from of (AI) technology. If (AI) producing sectors could grow, then it could lead to increase revenues and employment of (AI) technological professionals within these existing firms as well as the potential creation of entirely new economic activities to any countries' societies productivity improvement in existing sectors could be realized through faster and move efficient processes and decision making as well as increased (AI) technological knowledge and access to information available in societies easily.

In the future, if (AI) technology is an increasingly critical component of more products, it will become an integral part of necessary products of many people's lives. The extent of (AI)'s economy effort is also likely to vary from region to region, thought variation may be more dependent on the predominate economic activity of a region and the (AI) ability can influence economic activity, rather then the economic or developmental status of the regions. (AI) technology can move accessibility and can use source development to do international business between one country and another country.

So (AI) technology has the potential to give benefits to different income chooses and to bring significant gains to both developed and developing countries. For agricultural technology, (AI) has the potential to optimize food production around the world by analyzing agricultural regions and identifying what is necessary to improve crop yield. In total, (AI) technology gives greater economic impact to any countries agricultural regions if which implemented (AI) technology to grow crop , fruit etc. food production in the farms.

Investment in (AI) technology is such as capital investment to any countries' public or private enterprises. So, it will have large economic impact to the future . If the (AI) technology is reasonable invested to the different needs aspect by the public or private enterprises in the country. Then, it will have good economic impact to the country in the future. However, when (AI) technology is likely to affect both the productivity and employment components of economic growth in many sectors. Significant public debate has focused on projections of (AI)'s effect on the labor force. However, for instance, some researchers have argued that the rise of (AI) technology and automation will led to significant unemployment as capital is substituted for the low skillful labor. So, they point to the concern that the increasing sophistication of (AI) technology may balance skilled and semi-skilled workers and the reduce the size of the middle class. However, this is not a new argument, due to (AI) technology negatively affecting the labor force and leading to mass unemployment. Because the (AI) technology is the substitution of machinery for human labor. Although, employment in certain industries, has been reduced in the past due to technological advancement. For long term, the labor market has adapted to the introduction of new technology, giving rise to new jobs in new areas. (AI) technology may also be accomplished without a reduction to total employment in the long-term to some Asia countries, such as Hong Kong and Japan. Because Hong Kong and Japan many low skilled labor, e.g. security, cleaner who complaint that employers need them to work long time hours. (abnormal working hours) e.g. one day 12 to 15 working hour per day. Hence, if (AI) machine means invention technology success. Security or cleaning job can be worked from (AI) machine man in some hours every day in order to reduce the long time working hours cleaners or security workers, e.g. one (AI) machine man works 4 hours for cleaning or security job, one day as well as another cleaner or security labor only needs to work 8 hours one day. So total security or cleaning employers can employ 12 hours machine cleaners or security workers and human cleaners or security workers in one day. For long term benefit, Hong Kong or Japan every security or cleaning worker does not need to work 12 hours minimum working hours one day. They won't feel tried and bore and without private with whose families, so who will accept to do these cleaning or security jobs, even they can raise work efficient and performance when who feel happy and health. So, (AI) technology of machine man invention can raise low skillful labor efficiency and it can help them to avoid abnormal working hours demand in some busy work life countries, such as Hong Kong and Japan. Before, one Japan female labor feel unhappy to work, due to who often needs to work abnormal working hours for her employer and who has less sleeping and without any private time to enjoy her life with her families every day. So this abnormal working hours factor causes her to do commit suicide behavior, then she is die unlucky. So (AI) technology of machine man invention ought avoid abnormal working hours demand for employer in any countries in the future.

The most important occurrence to any employers, some researchers had attempted to do one experiment to find that private research and development , venture capital and public research and development investment all have strong net effect or economic growth with venture capital funding further having the strongest such effect from (AI) technology. The researchers hypothesize the venture capital investment contributes to economic growth through (AI) technology innovation and by the capacity of an economy to use existing (AI) technology knowledge to increase productivity. They predict the impacts of venture capital, business-research and development and public research and development can raise multi factor productivity from (AI) technology introduction.

Can (AI) technology influence the economic development to developing countries? The developing regions of the world contain most of natural resources. If one day, (AI) technology has invent one kind of machine man which can assist any gas or oil workers to seek any new oil/gas natural resource locations easily. I believe that (AI) technology can help these natural resource exploitation countries will gain economic benefit more easily. So, (AI) driven technology can be used to change to create any new opportunities to address poor management or resources and improve human well being, such as Africa Latin America and India can use (AI) technology machine man to seek any oil/gas natural resource countries exploitation activities to attempt to gain much economic benefits.

● Can AI help offices to reduce labor number

Nowadays, increases in capital and labor are no longer driving the levels of economic growth, such as (AI) technology. The ability of increase in capital investment and in labor of traditional drivers of production, have no longer to be enjoyed in most developed economies ,e.g. developed country, US, UK . However, artificial intelligence has the potential to overcome the physical limitation of capital and labor to avoid missing out on this opportunity. So, policy makers and business leaders must prepare for and work toward a future with artificial intelligence. They must do with the idea that (AI) is another simply method to enhance productivity method . Rather they must see (AI) as the tool that can transform thinking about how growth is created.

Economists have always thought of new technologies are as driving growth their ability to enhancing. It can replace labor and capital factor of production. So, it brings this question: What is the factor of production (AI) technology characteristics. They key factor is to see (AI) technology as a capital-labor .

(AI) can replicate labor activities at much greater scale and speed, and to even perform some tasks began the capabilities of human. For example, by using virtual assistants , 1000 legal documents can be reviewed in a matter of days instead of taking three people six moths to complete. Some (AI) technology may be one kind of factor of production in the future. For another example, people will work in workplace digitalization environment. So, in the future, working environment and information management are automated. Such as Konica camera sale company will use workplace digitalization. So , (AI) technology can provide workplace digitalization in order to raise productivity efficiency. (AI) technology will be one kind of production which is replaced by workplace digitalization and it will grow any organization productivity efficiently. Then, (AI) technology will assist overall social economy growth , due to productivity is raised and products can be produced in short time to prepare to sell in consumption market. So, time will be shortened to increase GDP growth fast for the development of (AI) technology countries.

What will be the development of (AI) technology and predictions concerning the future evolution? The computers and robots will develop conscious, intelligent and minds into humans, enhancing psychological and behavioral abilities and allowing for direct communication with (AI) minds. (AI) technology will be impacted human life by (AI) technology information communicative and environmental influence. A " world brain" and " world mind", this psychological system will be enhanced and enriched the capacities of both individual and collective cognition by (AI) technology of service industries.

(AI) technology with influence these human needs of service industries changes, such as , biological science, finance, entertainment, business, biological science, transportation, communication military etc. The personal computer evolution, the internet and the world wide web which exploded on the scene, linking business, homes, schools, social organizations which were a completely unpredicted phenomenon to influence human life. Kurzweil (1999) predicts that by 2029 year, most human communication will be with machines. According to Person, by 2100 year, there will be human machine convergence.

How can (AI) technology influence environmental protection to make benefits to farming economic growth? (AI) technology can be applied to predict how to solve environmental pollution challenge to avoid to damage any crop or vegetable or rice or fruit etc. food growth. Because environmental experts can gather global environmental pollution data from an environmental database to build a perform a systematic analysis from (AI) technology. The first step is this broad analysis can include understanding, statistical and data gathering techniques to obtain the relevant data, the correlation among the variables involved, and a list of possible models. The next step is to select a set of methods and models that cover all kinds of knowledge and functionalities needed for the decision making process. Once the models are selected, they must be fully implemented by means of machine learning , data mining, statistical or numerical technique. After that, those models must be integrated to build the whole EDSS. The EDSS must be tested to check its performance, accuracy, usefulness and reliability, both from the user's and (AI) technology/computer scientist's point of view. If these is any wrong feature in any development stage, such as model's integration, models' implementation, selection of models, database, problem analysis etc. the developers must come back in the update th required components. When the evaluation phase is all right, the EDSS is ready to be applied to the environment. The great contribution of artificial intelligence to EDSS the integration of several methods complementing the classical statistical models/simulation , statistical analysis, linear models, etc. and numerical models (control algorithms, optimization techniques etc.) .

This cooperation makes the resulting systems more reliable and powerful in coping with real world environment systems. Date interpretation has been a principal area of research in (AI) technology since the very beginning. The most demanding problem in the environmental assessment context. Knowledge representation permits the definition of the different types of data that the existing methods adapt to the process. There is also a lot of work to clean, repair and transform the huge available quantities of raw data. Apart from this, the availability of meta-information or background knowledge is required to guide the process. Data mining is multi-disciplinary: It covers expert systems, data based technology, statistics, data visualization and unsupervised machine learning. These techniques operate at the level of data and background information, where numerous and often incompatible new commensurate pieces of information from disparate sources have to be brought together (K. Fedra. 1994).

So, it seems that in the future, (AI) technology with the increasing maturity in particular those related to knowledge and engineering, new dimensions can be assisted to users in environmental decision making are available. For example, many environmental systems are characterized both by incomplete models and by limited data. Hence, in the future, (AI) technology will be applied to predict climate change to reduce crop or fruit etc. food agriculture challenge by climate change bad influence.

To understand how the manufacturing business must adapt to prosper in the technology, we need to understand how (AI) technology will change us to shape our daily habits to satisfy our expectation of products to how we shop and even the immediate of the entire process. For example, taxi services are in the crosshairs as on demand transportation services like, available of the touch of a smart phone button expand. In fact, Yellow lab, US country , san Francisco city's largest taxi company is filing for bankruptcy as the industry starts to change faster than almost anyone expected. However, at this point, its more than an app that is changing, some our taxi passengers renting taxi transportation to catch consumption behavior.

(AI) technology will influence digital economy for taxi passenger's individual customer experience, offering a growing renting taxi to catch of service and feedback opportunities when any one taxi passenger who chooses to use mobile phone app online tool to prepaid to rent any taxi more easily.

Also in the long term, (AI) technology can influence vehicles drive themselves of behavior. Already, companies like Google and GM are working on projects to bring fleets of autonomous vehicles to cities at the path of a button.

Moreover, this on-demand service model is beginning to appear across a much broader range of markets. For example , Amazon company is investing in its own fleet of trucks, planes and even drone at the same time as it pushes for same-day delivery of products. As some point, vehicles will be autonomous too. So, it seems that (AI) technique will influence any transportations choose to use digital autonomous driving technology in the future . For Amazon company case, it is not stopping of logistics. It is also aiming to automatically manage the supply of consumer home products with its recently launched Amazon replenishment service, Dash. Dash is a digital service that enables that connected derive to automatically order physical products from Amazon when supplies are running low. So, it seems (AI) technology will be applied to logistic function by digital technology method introduction in the future.

Hence autonomous vehicles will optimize industry supply chains and logistics operations through increased efficiency and flexibility. In fact, fully automated and lean supply chains will keep reduce load sizes and inventory by leveraging smart distribution technologies and smaller autonomous vehicles by machine man assistance. If Amazon continues to grow market share for online sales by reducing effort required by the consumer to place an order, when also contributing the almost immediate delivery of products to the doorstep. So, it will further fuel the trend toward on-demand derive. As Amazon company fuels the on-demand economy, consumers will expect immediacy in more parts of the digital economy. On top of speed, consumers increasing expect more personalization options.

So, (AI) technology will influence digital manufacturing, such as Amazon publishing to monitor every aspect of every process in real -time and communicating to self-optimized deep learning robotics, new methods of high volume and high customization will become possible. Then, as products merge into product platforms and even services, manufacturers have the opportunity to provide components and platforms used by smaller players. So, (AI) technology will influence manufacturing industry to choose automated SMI lines, robots installed, automation engineers.

Another future (AI) technology development can be applied to space science aspect, such as Automation engineering space in manufacturing process to achieve digital manufacturing benefits to any businesses in the future. Such as reducing cost, shortening manufacturing time, raising efficiency, shortening delivery products to client individual time. How can artificial intelligence give the need and advanced fast and evaluation methods benefits for space exploration? When US NASA (space exploration organization) achieves any space exploration missions, it will answer this question:

When is it useful to have a machine use (AI) technology to achieve a decision? After all, after millions of years of space exploration and rough 10,000 years of civilization, humans are usually quite good at making decisions in complex uncertain environments. Through, Johns Hoplains University's Applied Physical Lab. Research in (AI) technology enabled systems, which has identified three general use cases for (AI) technology to explore space mission:

First, for some tasks (AI) technology is more cost effectiveness than human. Second, (AI) technology is better suited than humans at solving some, but not all problems. Third, (AI) technology allows NASA organization's space exploration mission to develop machines that ate capable of responding faster than when a human is in the decision loop (D. Scheidt, 2012, A. Castano et. al. 2008).

So, the use of (AI) technology to enable science by observing the pace of rapidly evolving phenomena was demonstrated. It is more effectively coordinating and (AI) technology utilizing to earn economic benefits to use for space exploration mission.

However, (AI) technology also have current risk for space exploration. Today (AI) technology is immature and requires further development to reach its potential. For instance, the (AI) technology algorithms that detected the dust derive could not have identified whether the Martain weather represented a threat to the cover. Also it can not yet use instrument input to determine what, where and how to autonomously make the next space science measurement. An equally important factor limiting (AI)'s deployment is that lacks the methodology and technology to effectively test (AI) technology. So, the challenge will testing (AI) enabled system is how (AI) performance can be measured. It would be NASA organization's difficulty to find (AI) technology to develop to carry on researching any space exploration missions in the future. However, (AI) technology will be a good economic benefit choice for space exploration mission in the future.

Artificial intelligent office create what benefits

● what is artificial intelligent technological office

Can artificial intelligent technology apply to office to reduce energy consumption ? The Artificial Intelligence & Technology Office (AITO), the Department of Energy's center for artificial intelligence, will accelerate the delivery of AI-enabled capabilities, scale the Department-wide development of AI, synchronize AI applications to advance the agency's core missions, and expand public and private sector strategic partnerships, all in support of American AI leadership. I believe that when AI is applied to office, it can bring these several actural benefits to offices below:

1. ON REDUCING ENERGY CONSUMPTION ASPECTThe world's transition to clean renewable energy, such as solar, wind, and biofuels, relies on our actions. We must engage in this change by optimizing the power consumed by our homes, buildings, and machines. Indeed, studies have shown that continuously adjusting the latter's operations, and implementing energy-efficiency strategies, could be very beneficial. Energy use may be reduced by 30%. But how can it be achieved? Leveraging artificial intelligence is the answer.

However, in real life, it only refers to computational systems that behave intelligently, applying advanced algorithms on large sets of data. These smart devices embody AI's predictive power and flexibility to changing environments and changing goals. Indeed, AI can help reduce energy consumption in several ways:

Catch operational strays:

Catching operational strays or energy leaks quickly is the aim of efficient real-time energy management. AI systems can predict when these leaks happen, especially for large office buildings where equipment might deviate from optimum settings. This would hence reduce energy-waste, save money for owners and tenants, protect equipment from wear and tear, and maintain better buildings.

Breakdown the energy consumption:

Machine Learning techniques can detect consumption behaviors and energy use patterns. Such meaningful insights can, therefore, help utility companies build better client segments, and personalize customer offers with relevant information. Additionally, households can directly benefit from these insights -if well presented to them, by regaining control after understanding their own consumption (and electricity bill!).

Find the best place for solar energy placement:

The crucial part about the deployment of solar energy solutions is the cost related to their installation. However, these costs will be drastically reduced if businesses target the most interesting prospects and areas. Using machine learning along with data relevant to tree shading, income, home size, energy costs, rebates, incentives, and roof-orientation is key to cost and risk control. Indeed, leveraging this information helps locate the best area in terms of energy performance. AI and machine learning enable various business opportunities. They empowered the first waves of startups to develop new products meant to save more energy. Nevertheless, there are some standing issues to be tackled:

Data acquisition:

Governments and utilities are deploying smart meters all over the world as these lines are written*. This will permit access to more interesting data in the future. However, considerable efforts are required to cover wider areas and develop specific machine-learning algorithms. An example of the latter would be non-supervised & semi-supervised learning, which can predict energy-consumption levels even for the homes lacking smart meters.

The reluctance of the industry:

The energy industry is very conservative. Its business model did not change since Thomas Edison –as Alex Laskey, co-founder of Opower, asserted in a Ted Talk! "Utilities are still rewarded when their customers waste energy", he said. To use AI applications and aim for energy efficiency, utilities must become more than energy providers. They must be convinced that being user-centric and "smart" is where profitability lies in the "smart grid" era.

The arrival of electric vehicles:

As more electric vehicles enter the market (their number is doubling each year!), questions about managing their battery charging cycles arise. Considered as the largest home appliance ever, their identification while plugged in the grid is crucial to optimally manage energy demand and supply.

● Why does AI help offices to save energy ?

Hence, AI will be future offices new energy consumption saving tool. It can help any offices to save energy. As with all emerging technological trends, some elements of artificial intelligence are hyped out of proportion, some elements are ahead of their time, and some even incite fear. However, there remains some truth beneath the hype, cycles and buzzwords. Advancements in AI stand to benefit the energy sector but come with own limitations and practical concerns.

Currently, AI, Machine Learning, and their other counterparts Deep Learning, Reinforcement Learning etc, have seen wide coverage in a variety of industries. But what do all these terms mean? AI is a broad term and its scope varies but the idea is simple – adaptive intelligence displayed independently by a machine, in which the behaviour is not necessarily pre-determined, but which adapts to data inputs.

AI in informal settings is used interchangeably with Machine Learning (ML), but in reality, ML is a subset of AI. Deep Learning and Reinforcement Learning are promising areas within ML. Within AI and next to ML there are the fields of robotics, speech recognition, computer vision, etc., which are key building blocks towards enabling machine intelligence. ML is the use of statistics to give computers the ability to learn from data. This differentiation is key because fast advances in ML have led to the sudden interest in AI worldwide. The initial set of improvements have been in the underlying algorithms and data architectures, but the current key improvements are just two: data and computation.

Developments in data are driven by smartphone uptake and improvements in sensors, supported by revolutionary breakthroughs in data communications and data storage technologies. This has made many more datasets available than ever before, which allows for in-depth scrutinization enabling more accurate predictions to be made. The developments seen in computation can be attributed to dramatic increases in processing power, enabling algorithms to tackle many parameters simultaneously and conduct the same amount of computation in parallel rather than in sequence, saving a great deal of time.

What is AI/ML used for?

Most ML methods are suited to tackling two key problems: prediction type problems and classification type problems. Prediction type problems include 'can I predict when this equipment will fail?' (If so, I can deploy maintenance before failure to ensure the plant doesn't grind to a halt, while saving on unnecessary maintenance). Classification type problems include 'is this customer different from another, based on the data I have from them?' (If so, I can further study the differences and maybe deploy a new marketing program to retain them). The key requirement to enable these ML predictions has been the need for clean and useful datasets. For this reason, the ML method that has been showing the most potential recently is Deep Learning, a type of model which can extract complex patterns and sequences in a dataset.

In challenging areas such as speech recognition and image recognition, Deep Learning models have seen more success than traditional rules-based approaches or detailed expert systems and has led to a marked increase in accuracy of the prediction, well beyond what was possible before. Some popular examples of products which use Deep Learning (amongst other models) are Siri, Cortana, and Google Translate for speech/text recognition. The Google Translate model, for example, was trained on large amounts of EU and UN documents online which provide the same text professionally translated into different languages.

The most promising area with AI and ML is Reinforcement Learning, which involves training software agents towards a certain goal through rewards – in a sense mimicking how humans learn. This, when combined with Deep Learning, has led to powerful strides towards accurate prediction systems and is the key algorithm being used to drive autonomous vehicles.

A particularly interesting example of Reinforcement learning is AlphaGo, which was the first computer program able to beat a high-ranking professional player in the complex board game Go. It did this through playing against itself and other repeatedly in order to know how to make the right move out of the billions of combinations possible. In short, the core idea of ML methods is that, as long as the data and computational power are available, it is possible to augment and even automate decision-making by creating some sort of expert system.

The future of these expert systems lies not only in enabling automation, but also in aiding complex decisions. Nowadays, computational power is easy to acquire (even for a short-term basis), and common algorithms are reasonably well known. The major investment required is in the form of time needed to acquire and assemble data, remove any mistakes from it, and assess different algorithms to see which one delivers the best performance. In energy, there are several interesting examples in both the retail and the commercial space:

· Fault prediction and dynamic maintenance: This is one of the clearest uses of AI, and enables operators to predict equipment failures. It does this by using sensor data from various units, and significantly reduce their costs of downtime and maintenance. A start-up, Verv, is offering a meter device which identifies individual home appliances and tries to predict faults and alert when devices are accidentally left on.

· Investment optimisation: BP's venture arm invested in an AI start-up called Beyond Limits, enabling them to dig through seismic images and geological models to increase the chances of success when drilling wells.

· Energy efficiency: Deepmind, a part of Google, has championed the use of Reinforcement Learning to reduce energy use in their data centres by a claimed 15 per cent. The model learnt by looking at years of operational data and then issued changes to individual units.

· Better prediction: Deepmind has also recently announced talks with National Grid to better forecast demand of the system, with the stated goal of reducing the entire country's energy usage by 10 per cent.

· Trading: Origami Energy uses machine learning to predict asset availability and market prices in near real time, enabling them to successfully bid into the Frequency Response markets. Pöyry is also exploring a deep learning algorithm to support trading and dispatch decisions for generation assets in the prompt trading markets, focusing on the issue 'when should I commit a trade' (to maximise the option value of flexible capacity).

· Retail: Retailers are using ML to understand patterns of customer behaviour, to attract and retain customers and even to predict bill (non)-payment. Customer call centres are being fronted by algorithms which chat to customers (verbally or online) and deal with queries verbally.

· Customers: For customers, AI solutions are also gaining traction, and many retailers are offering these systems as part of an integrated package. Devices such as Amazon's Alexa enable the customer to seamlessly interact with their thermostat and control systems (such as Centrica's Hive). This increasing customer interaction with the device leads to the development of a more personalised usage profile, which reduces bills for the consumer and helps the energy provider to accurately forecast demand.

Despite all the upsides, AI comes with many caveats. What happens if there is a low volume of data available for the ML model to learn from? Can it contextualise between two similar tasks and transfer learnings from one to the other? How can AI systems be protected against false (perhaps maliciously-introduced) data? As some of these models are essentially black boxes, can the model users understand why the model took a particular action? Will the AI systems learn to collude or break through regulatory ringfences? Can the model take the right decision when it faces a new unforeseen environment? And, as decisions are increasingly driven by AI outcomes, will the underlying system converge, or will the outcomes be unstable? To some degree, Reinforcement Learning coupled with intelligent model design with safety constraints and external controls can allay many of these concerns (this is being used for Autonomous Vehicle technology).

Techniques will develop to combine historic-based AI outcomes with anticipated future changes in the fundamentals (e.g. new interconnection, changes in market rules), but these questions will persist, e.g. how should a car react in an earthquake if it never had a dataset under earthquake conditions? As the standards of AI decision support improve, the interface with humans must adapt. Initially, humans must learn to trust the systems, even though the results cannot fully be explained. Techniques will be found to blend humans' anticipation of the future with existing (historical) data to augment today's algorithms, in what might be termed 'augmented artificial intelligence' (in which the AI is augmented by human knowledge, not the other way around).

And ultimately, as the algorithms become more robust and are given more autonomy to act without human intervention, we need to ensure that appropriate monitoring, alerts and controls are put in place. That being said, AI or rather ML as it stands, is a powerful tool for prediction and classification problems, as long as the data to learn from exists. In non-critical business applications, ML is uncovering value in almost every application where past predictive data exists. The caveats must be put in context: human behaviour and existing prediction methods are far from perfect, and AI should not be compared with an impossible benchmark. For now, AI/ML coupled with better analytics, improvement in sensors and robotics can help automate the small directed issues entirely and let us focus on the unstructured problems of tomorrow. So, AI will be applied to help any offices to avoid long time electricity waste problem. It will be one electricity sense machine tool to inform any staffs when and why and how that they do not need to spend extra electricity waste to use to offices any time. Robotic will be one assistant to inform manager how he/she can avoid to spend too much electricity to waste to use. Then office can reduce much electricity expense in long time.

● On Artificial Intelligence In The Workplace: How AI Is Transforming Your Employee Experience Benefit Aspect

AI can help manager to interview and training benefit both aspect, artificial intelligence (AI) is quickly changing just about every aspect of how we live our lives, and our working lives certainly aren't exempt from this. Soon, even those of us who don't happen to work for technology companies (although as every company moves towards becoming a tech company, that will be increasingly few of us) will find AI-enabled machines increasingly present as we go about our day-to-day activities.

On Shorten interview time aspect

From how we are recruited and on-boarded to how we go about on-the-job training, personal development and eventually passing on our skills and experience to those who follow in our footsteps, AI technology will play an increasingly prominent role.Here's an overview of some of the recent advances made in businesses that are currently on the cutting-edge of the AI revolution, and are likely to be increasingly adopted by others seeking to capitalize on the arrival of smart machines. Before we even set foot in a new workplace, it could soon be a fact that AI-enabled machines have played their part in ensuring we're the right person for the job.

AI pre-screening of candidates before inviting the most suitable in for interviews is an increasingly common practice at large companies which make thousands of hires each year, and sometimes attract millions of applicants. Pymetricsprovides tools which use a series of "games" based on principles of neuroscience to assess candidates before they are asked in for an interview. It works by assessing cognitive and emotional features of the candidate, while specifically avoiding demographic biases based on their gender, socioeconomic status, or race. This is done by matching candidates' performance against that of existing employees who have succeeded in the roles that are being recruited for. If it finds that they may not be a particularly good fit for that role, it might recognize another role they would be suitable for and recommend they instead apply for that one. Another company providing these services is Montage, which claims that 100 of the Fortune 500 companies have used their AI-driven interviewing tool. It enables businesses to carry out on-demand text interviewing, automated scheduling, and reduce the impact of unconscious biases on the recruitment process. When it comes to onboarding, AI-enabled chatbots are the current tool of choice, for helping new hires settle into their roles and get to grips with the various facets of the organizations they've joined. Multinational consumer goods manufacturer Unilever uses a chatbot called Unabot, that employs natural language processing(NLP) to answer employees' questions in plain, human language. Advice is available on everything from where they can catch a shuttle bus to the office in the morning, to how to deal with HR and payroll issues.

On-the-job training

Of course, learning doesn't end once you've settled into your role, and AI technology will also play a part in ongoing training for most employees in the future. It will also assist with the transfer of skills from one generation to the next – as employees move on to other companies or retire, it can help to ensure that they can leave behind the valuable experience they've gained for others to benefit from, as well as take it with them.

Engineering giant Honeywellhas developed tools which utilize augmented and virtual reality (AR/VR) along with AI, to capture the experience of work and extract "lessons" from it which can be passed on to newer hires. Employees wear AR headsets while carrying out their daily tasks. These capture a record of everything the engineer does, using image recognition technology, which can be played back, allowing trainees or new hires to experience the role through VR. Information from the video imagery is also being used to build AR tools which provide real-time feedback while engineers carry out their job – alerting them to dangers or reminding them to carry out routine tasks when they are in a particular place or looking at a particular object.

Augmented workforce

One of the reasons that the subject of AI in the workplace makes some people uncomfortable is because it is often thought of as something that will replace humans and lead to job losses. However, when it comes to AI integration today, the keyword is very much "augmentation" – the idea that AI machines will help us do our jobs more efficiently, rather than replace us. A key idea is that they will take over the mundane aspects of our role, leaving us free to do what humans do best – tasks which require creativity and human-to-human interaction. Just as employees have become familiar with tools like email and messaging apps, tools such as those provided by PeopleDocor Betterworkswill play an increasingly large part in the day-today workplace experience. These are tools which can monitor workflows and processes and make intelligent suggestions about how things could be done more effectively or efficiently. Often this is referred to as robotic process automation (RPA). These tools will learn to carry out repetitive tasks such as arranging meetings or managing a diary. They will also recognize when employees are having difficulty or spending too long on particular problems, and be ready to step in to either assist or if the job is beyond something a bot is capable of doing itself, suggest where human help can be found.

Surveillance in the workplace

Of course, there's a potential dark side to this encroachment of AI into the workplace that's likely to leave some employees feeling distinctly uncomfortable. According to a Gartner survey, more than 50% of companies with a turnover above $750 million use digital data-gathering tools to monitor employee activities and performance. This includes analyzing the content of emails to determine employee satisfaction and engagement levels. Some companies are known to be using tracking devices to monitor the frequency of bathroom breaks, as well as audio analytics to determine stress levels in voices when staff speak to each other in the office.

Technology even exists to enable employers to track their staff sleeping and exercise habits. Video game publisher Blizzard Activision recently unveiled plansto offer incentives to staff who let them track their health through Fitbit devices and other specialized apps. The idea is to use aggregated, anonymized data to identify areas where the health of the workforce as a whole can be improved. However, it's clear to see that being monitored in this way might not sit particularly well with everyone. Workplace analytics specialists Humanyzeuse staff email and instant messaging data, along with microphone-equipped name badges, to gather data on employee interactions. While some may consider this potentially intrusive, the company says that this can help to protect employees from bullying or sexual harassment in the workplace.

Workplace Robots

Physical robots capable of autonomous movement are becoming commonplace in manufacturing and warehousing installations, and are likely to be a feature of many other workplaces in the near future.

Mobility experts Segwayhave created a delivery robot which can navigate through workplace corridors to make deliveries directly to the desk. Meanwhile, security robots such as those being developed by Gamma 2could soon be a common site, ensuring commercial properties are safe from trespassers.

Racing for a space in the office car park could also become a thing of the past if solutions developed by providers such as ParkPlusbecome commonplace. Their robotic parking assistants may not match our traditional idea of how a robot should look, but consist of automated "shuttle units" capable of moving vehicles into parking bays which would be too small for humans to manually park in – meaning more vehicles can fit into a smaller space. Hence, future AI ought may help any offices to create safe and comfortable and high efficiency and avoiding energy waste working environment.

The relationship between AI and climate change to influence society
● How AI develops digital agriculture

Nowadays, our society is influences by bad climate, due to manufacturers pollute our Earth air and water. So, climate change brings disadvantages to influence our future living or poor standard of living. Can artificial intelligence help our climate to be better? How to apply artificial intelligent technology to let human does not afraid climate change's negative impaact to our living? How artificial intelligence can keep balance to manufacturers' behaviors in order to avoid air and water pollution . I shall explain as below: In the agriculture and food value, chain, firstly, agricultural machinery, agochemicals , plant breeding industries, then crops, livestock agriculture development. It will bring either bio-based products and bioenergy industries or food processing industries. Next, the wholesale and distribution to warehouses, retailers, restaurants and final to the consumers to satisfy their demand and consumption.

However, in all these processes, farmers may pollute the water, or food manufacturing process may be polluted. If in these food manufacturing process, farmers or food manufacturers , food wholesalers can apply artificial intelligent technology to manufacture their food in order to avoid to pollute water or food is avoided to be polluted. Then , our food consumers may buy more health food to reduce sickness risk. Then, artificial intelligence can help us to reduce social and environmental challenges for agriculture aspect, such as farmers can have incomes and working conditions, avoidance to scarcity of natural resources (e.g. fertilizers, oil for energy).

Agriculture how contributes to climate change: Agriculture is among the greatest contributes to global warming (methane, nitrous oxide, carbon, dioxide emissions), also from the conversion of non-agricultural land (e.g. forect) into agricultural land, with other post-production processes (food processing, distribution , consumption). The impact of climate change on agriculture may bring negative effect on the both aspects:

Decreases of productivity, due to changes in temperatures and rainfall, reduced water resources, increases diseases as well as changes in the social , such as preservation of the environment, consumers' demand for local, organic or low-input to do products. When, farmers and food manufacturers can apply artificial intelligent technology to bring smarter farming for productivity raise, mitigration, and adapt to climate change: New agronomical praactices, more resilient crop varieties and species, improved irrigiation practices, increasing agroforestry, developing biocontrol and agroecology as well as developing technologies , such as biotechbology and digital agriculture. For example, digital agriculture is lased to apply robotics collect store, analyze and share electronic data along the agricutlure food value chain. So, robotics can help farmers to raise crop, fruit etc. food productivities and improve efficiency and avoid pollution to water, air and foods themselves.

Moreover, new AI tools for farmers to optimize management of resources can improve crop quality and quantity and remain production in a changing climate, ditigal integration of potentially all food process stages, from refining crop genetics to managing transportation logistics and B2C relationship . So, robotics can help food distributors or warehouses to deliver food to any places efficiently in short time. So, artificial intelligence can have more accurate and analytical ability, such as observing , resoning , acting in order to make decisions and prediction more accurate than human.

Artificial intelligence will be a core technology to digital agriculture: Low cost monitoring, internet of things, satellite , sensors, tractors and farm machineries, robotics can make decision and planning from observation to disgnosis to recommendation to final action stage efficiently. Hence, future in farm industry, robotic can be applied to digital agriculture to give decision, planning observation, recommendation benefits to let farmers to do more accurate action. It is one farmers assistant to help them to predict when climate is good or bad in order to decide when it right time to growing crop, fruit on farm in order to raise food productivities as well avoid pollution is occurred easily during growing food process for farmers or manufacturing food process for food manufacturers or distribution.

● How AI can predict , mitigrate and adapt to the impacts of climate change?

On predicting climate change aspect, AI refers to computer systems that " CAN SENSE THEIR ENVIRONMENT, THINK, LEARN, AND ACT IN REPONSE TO WHAT THEY SENSE AND THEIR PROGRAMMED OBJECTIVES." AI processes who give machines the ability to learn from experience as they take in more data to perform tasks like humans. These processes include learning (the acquisition of information and rules for using the information), reasoning (using rules to reach approximate or definite conclusions) and self-correction. AI can be applied to predict when climate change to cause bad weather occurrence to avoid our houses are damages or accidents occurrence to cause hurt or death to our lifes.

Climate change will bring adverse effects in the physical environment or biota, which have significant deleterious effects on the productivity of nature and managed ecosystems, on the operation of socio-economic systems and on human health and welfare. Hence, on a predictable climate change tool to (AI) can help us to implement strategies, initiatives and measures of individuals, communities and organizations to reduce the damages of natural and human systems to the present and expected effects of climate change. It involves taking practical actions to manage risks from climate impacts, protect communities and strengthen economy, such as predicting when is the bad climate time to avoid grow fruit or crop to cause food proeuctivities loss in the wrong time for farmers.

● What is AI predicting climate change process?

Hence, Ai is a big data computers have given us access to vast amounts of data, both structured (in data bases and spreadsheets) and unstructured (such as text, audio, and images) . All of these world, AI assisted processing of this informatin allows us to use this data to discover historical patterns, predict more efficiently, make more effective recommendations. Accelerating technologies , such as cloud computing and graphics processing units have made cheaper and faster the managing of large volumes of data, social media platforms have fundamentally changed the way people interact. This increased connectivity has accelerated the spread of information and encouraged knowledge sharing, leading to the emergence of a collective intelligence, including open-source communities developing AI climate change prediction tool and sharing apps. Hence, Ai can predict when temperature changes to influence any crops , fruits grow easily. When farmers can predict temperature when changes to the worest time. Then, they can make the decision to avoid to grow any kinds of crops or fruits or vegetables on farms in order to avoid food loss risk.

● Why does AI can avoid industralization pollution?

Industralization leds climate change to cause environmental problems. For example, climate change, unsafe levels of air pollution, the depletion of fishing stocks, toxims in rivers and soils, overflowing levels of waste on land and in the ocean, loss of biodiversity and deforestation can be traced to industrialization . However, (AI) invention, it will be one kind of new technolgical tool to avoid the disadvantages cause from industrialization.

In fact, (AI) is having a significant impact on society, changing the way se work, live and interact. AI is helping the world diagnose diseases and develop climical pathways. AI could also be developed to support the creation of distributed, " offgrid" water and energy resources, to improve climate modelling, or to avoid natural disaster cause. As AI is the electricity avoid for Fourth industrial revaluation, its potential would help to create benefitical outcomes for humanity and the planet inhabit.

However, AI can help us to solve climate change challenges, they may occurs in the future, such as avoiding global average temperatures in 2100 year are still expected to be 3 degree above pre-industrial levels, well above the targets to avoid the worst impacts of climate changem , avoiding Earth will rise to 50% temperature by the end ot the century, reducing the resulting ocean acidification and warming are leading to unprecedented damage to fish stocks and corals.

The Earth industrial revalution . AI is a term for computer systems that can sense their environment , think, learn and act in response to what they sense and their progrommed objectives. AI is expected to have the deepest impact, to avoid climate changes poor development aspect, instead of our daily tasks aspect. Hence, AI will be the best climate change prediction tool to help human to avoid as well as pollution serious to damage our nature environment as well as to bring food shortage challenge , due to lacking farming land supply , bad climate factors cause . Hence, AI technology and avoiding poor climate change occurrence. They have close relationship . If we can continue to invent AI to apply on this improving climate change aspect, human will have safe place to continue to live.

Robotic creates new jobs or reduces old jobs

● Why does robotics reduce old jobs only?

Future robotic continue invention, whether it will any employers feel need to create any new job positions in order to cooperate with human workers to raise efficiency or improve performance or existing old job positions will be replaced by robotics. Consequently, it can bring either creating any new jobs and reduces unemployment ratio or ole job positions are replaced by robotics , and increases unemployment ratio in our societies. I shall attempt to follow present robotic development trend to explain whether robotics can create new job chance or reduces old job change in our future societies as below:

Some scientists evaluate that the number of robots in use world wide multiplied three- fold over the past two decades to 2025 million. Trends suggest the global stock of robots will multiply even faster in the next 20 yeats, reaching as many as 20 million by 2030 , with 14 million in China alone. It seems that the rise of the robots will boost productivity and economic growth. it ought lead too, to the creation of new jobs in exist industries in a process of creative destruction.

However, existing business models across many sectors will be seriously disrupted. And tens of million of existing jobs will be lost, with human workers displaced by robotic at an increasing rat as robots become steadily more job losses will vary greatly across countries and regions with a disproportionate on lower-skilled workers and on poor local economies. The impact will aggravate social and economic stresses from unemployment and income ineqaulity.

In our societies, robotics will bring lower income regions are more at risk, because the great displacement won't be evenly distributed around the world, the negative effects of robotization are disproportionately felt in the lower- income regions of the global 's major economies on average, a new robot displaces nearly twice of the same country. For example, if China big city shanghai, high income regions have many robotics to work. Then, the high income region people's income will be influenced to reduced , because their skills, e.g. manufacturing skills can be replaced by robotics. But if China's low income region, e.g. small cities employers like to use robotics in manufacturing industries. hen, the low skillful workers will be replaced by robotics. So, low skillful workers in the low income regions, they will be fried or unemployed by robotic's manufacturing participation to their old manufacturing jobs. So, robotics will may cause many low skillful workers unemployment ratio rises in China's low income region, if many low income regions chinese employers choose to apply many robotics to replace low skillful workers in factories. Although, it is possible that robotics can help Chinese manufacturing industries to raise also increase society, when many manufacturing industries apply robotics to replace workers in possible. When robotics may replace them to do their jobs in factories . Consequently, China won't have created any new occupation or job chance, e.g. transport, construction and maintenance, and office and administration work , when robotics are applied to automation. China's preparing for and responding to the social impact of automation will be a defining challenge to China's future society, when many industries apply robotics automatin works. Then, the low skillful workers job chance will be influenced to reduce and their job chance will be replaced by robotic or the high skillful workers. Although, today 90% of all robots used are found in factories and they are referred to as industrial robots. Also robotics are slowly finding their way into warehouses, laboratories , even power plants, hospitals and even outer space. Many employers feel that robotics can bring these advantages: Robots never get sick or need to rest, so they can work 24 hours, a day, 7 days a week, when the task required would be dangerous for a person, they can be do the work instead . Robots won't have negative emotion, it means that they do not feel bored. So, the work that is repetitive and unrewarding is of no problem for a robot. So, basing on above factors, it is possible that many human's job task, even occupations will be replaced by robotics. Then, when many various industrial applicatins of robots. Them, these human workers industrial tasks will be replaced by robotics, such as material transfer, machine loading, spot welding, spray coating, material removal, cutting opertions, assembling operations, part inspection, part sorting, part cleaning, part polishing, and a dozen more specialized tasks. Consequently, in our societies, many low -skilled workers' tasks will be replaced by robotics. They will face unemployment chance when global manufacturing industries decide to apply robotics to replace human workers in factories. Then, these factories tasks will disappear . For example, a more flexible automation technology which takes in account frequent changes in production is needed for thies category of manufactured parts. Hence, with the development of industrial tool loading and unloading machine tools are the major applications of robots. Robots are utilised to load and unload machine tools into (a) a robot tending a single machine and (b) a robot serving machine .

Hence, in future global manufacturing industries trend to develop industrial robots to replace traditional machine automation manufacturing technology . Then, factories won't need workers control machine to operate to manufacture, because industrial robots can do human workers' similar or same working behavior , even their manufacturing performance can be excellent to compare human workers performance in factories. Then, global factories low skillful rebotics. Consequently, low skilled factory workers will lose factory manufacturing jobs.

Some scientises and economists also predict about the risk of job autmation in future developing and developed countries both , such as:

About 14% jobs are highly automatable . Another 32% of jobs could face substantial chance in how they are carried out; automation mostly affects the manufacturing industry and agriculture, but some service sector jobs are highly automatable for young people as sudent jobs and entry-level positions have a higher risk of automation than jobs held by older workers. So, when any industries implement robotic automation. Then, many young technological students will feel difficult to find high technological job in labor market, because many employers will accept robotics to replace human workers to work in any high technological manufacturing industries, e.g. computer , vehicle, home appliance, working machines, warming machines, air condition, radio, television etc. technological products manufacturing performance to compare human high technological product manufacturing workers. Their manufacturing speed, efficiency, errors or manufacturing accident will be reduced to the lowest level to compare human workers. So, future any low technogical and high technological new manufacturing industries will trend to accept industrial robotic automation to replace traditional old industries human workers and machines automation working model. Consequently, the unemployment ratio to high technological and low technological industries to be accepted to apply to replace human workers in factories. There has been considered public debate about the extent of job destruction and whether automation and digitalisation are leading to mass technological unemplyment in which many jobs will be done by computers ans robots.

It is one new technological task change to manufacture industry. In future, factory workers can be replaced by computers as well as traditional old machines can be replaced by robotics. Hence, " artificial intelligent factories " will be caused when industrial robotics can be developed to apply to do any simple, even complex tasks in factories, when industrial robotic technological development will be achieved to the mature stage. Then, any high technological and low technological manufacturing jobs will be replaced by robotics.

Our societies will lose many low and high technological manufacturing occupations. Moreover, robotic development will influence any countries universities' traditional computer subjects to change " robotic industrial development subject" to change " robotic industrial development subjects" to let students to prepare how to control robotics to work in factories to change to let stuents own how controllinf artificial intelligence or robotics. When they own this kind of new skill. Then, they can find jobs in high technological product manufacturing industries more easily.

In health industry, future many hospitals will apply robotics to replace health care workers tasks. Future, medical robotics, health care robotics, assistive robotics, rehabilitatin robotics, surgical robotics, health design, health information technology, etc. different kinds of functions to robotics will be invented to replace health care workers in any hospitals or medical care organizations. Robotics can do more excellent performance to serve people who are ill or injured in hospitals. Hospital robotics may enact this change with effectors which can move the robot (locomotion) or objects in the hospital environment (maniipulation). Moreover, hospital robots typically use seneor data to make decisions. They can vary in their degree of autonomy, from fully autonomius to fully teleogerated, though most modern systems have mixed initiative or shared autonomy. Most broadly, robotic technology includes affiliated systems, such as related sensors, algorithms or processing data etc. Hence, future hospital robots mahy replace health workers to do their tasks in hospitals robotic some technology has been used for physical and cognitive rehabiliation. Surgery, telemedicine, drug delivery and patient management . Moreover, robots have been need across a range of environment, including hospitals, clinics, homes, schools, and mursing homes and in both urban and rural areas.

Hence, it implies that future some kinds of medical occupatins or tasks will be replaced to medical robotics . Then, some medical industry workers will also face unemployment chance, when medical robotics can serve patients to let them to let better performance or more satisfactory to compare nurses or medical occupation workers.

● How robotics impact to our future social change ?

On conclusion, I feel robotics will influence our future social several change in several aspects: As a consequence, robot-using industry influences negative effect on factory workers employment, but it brings positive machine producers benefit from any positive effect on employment, because robotics may be used 24 hours, 7 days and none bad emotion to influence poor working performance, inefficiency, low productivities , none salary expenditure to employers .

In fact, the robot adoption can lead to an increase in non automated tasks, and consumption . This determines higher demand and increase in employment. In general, in the case of AI , (artificial intelligence), it can serve as a platform to create new tasks in many service industries, e.g. hotel cleaning service, washing service, shopping centers' security service, instead general customer service tasks, in professional service tasks, they may include teacher education, professional assistant draft legal document, accounting tasks etc.

Finally, Higher production and enlarged consumption translate into higher demand and employment. So, future robotic ought not influence service industry's unemployment ratio increases. Otherwise, it is needed to train many service staffs to learn how to cooperate with robotic to improve service performance in any services environment, such as hotel cleaning room service tasks, washing washing cups , plates in kitchens , hotel serving workers need to learn how to cooperate service robotics to serve clients satisfactory. In shopping centers, managers need to learn how to cooperate with security robotics or reception robotics to let shoppers feel comfortable to go to shopping in shopping centers. Hospital medical workers also need to learn how to cooperate with medical robotics to serve patients to let them to feel more care satisfactory feeling. Hence, service industry workers will need to learn more new robotic controlling technique in order to improve service performance.

SIX

LEARNING HUMAN BEHAVIORS BRING WHAT ECONOMIC INFLUENCES

Human Behavioral network job brings social economic benefits

What does human network job mean ? Why may human network job be popular? Why human network job behavior may influence economy ?
Nowadays internet is popular to use. We can apply internet to find data , search any new things, even earn money. Why does internet
may become human network job source. For example, e-publish may be one kind of new human network job. Any authors may apply internet
channel to help them to sell electronic or paper books from e-publisher web store. They may apply facebook, you tub etc. any online
channel to promote themselves new books to let new readers to know whether when they may buy themselves favourable new topic books to read from electronic publisher web store.

Thus, future electronic publisher industry may help any authors to build internet network platform to help them to sell and promote
ot advertise their any one new electronic or paper book topic to let global any one reader to choose to buy their any new topic books from electronic publisher web store easily and conveniently. However, it implies that electronic network platform author may be one kind of future new human network job in our societies.

How electronic network platform author job may bring economy benefit in macro economy view? A person can have few friends, contacts and still be very influential if these few

friends and contacts are themselves highly influential, e.g. one author must not need to know any one reader in global society. When they like to choose any electronic books from electronic internet network platform. They may become the author's any one topic book buyer, when they feel the author's any one topic book is fun and attract they make decision to buth the strange author whose the topic book from electronic book publisher's platform web store conventiently in short time. Although, they are strangers, they do not know themselves , but the reader can understand what it way that made Google from writing platofrm to create new creative mind and typing network job method to replace traditional hand writing book method for global authors. It will be one kind of new human network writing job.

Hence, global any one reader can apply an innovative search engine , such as google.com to find whether whom author personal new topic books are value to read from internet.

Then, the electroniuc publisher's web store may be new book store platform sale network to help the author to sell many electronic or paper books from electronic network platform

in short time. So, internet may be future new network plaform to help global any one author to create network writing job absolutely. Furthermore, internet may be popular social media

to help any one author to build goold relationship between his/her readers. It is one kind of new network, human network job. New authors do not need to buy many paper books to prepare to put in any one book shop warehouse. Their every book can print on demand to reduce out of book stock in any one book shop. They may choose to sell either electronic books or paper books both from any one book publisher web store. So, electronic network platform may be one kind of good writing channel to help human authors to create income and it can also

help authors to bring new creative mind and new topic fun content books to let readers to know and buy to read from electronic publisher network platform.

Why does human behavior may be one kind of new human network job to bring global economic advantages. ALthough, it may be free income or without inocme, but the person does the network behavior, his/her behavior may be bring advantages to influence many other people's health. For this case, when a worker in a coffee shop in an airport gets a vaccination aganinst the flu, it does not only helps him or her stay healthy, but also helps the many travellers who might otherwise have been inflected if that workers caught the flu.

So, the externality , the result implies the vaccination of even a part of a community conveys benefits to the whole community. For example, governments pay special attention

to the vaccinations of school children, teachers, health mothers, and the elderly, categories of people particularly susceptible not only to catching, but also to transmitting a disease.

It is not accidential that governments are heavily involved with vaccination . When there are externalities, free market, fail to persuade individual incentives with society's

their the worker's decision of whether to get a vaccine ends up attracting whether other people get sick. The workers might not

fully take all these other people's potential suffering into account when making her or his vaccination decision.

As Stanford University does many suggestions, understand this and tries to help them make the right decisions and so providers free flu vaccines for its staff and students.

Small pockets of unvaccinated individuals can allow a disease to gain a spread more widely well-being. For example, parent weighing the costs and benefits of a vaccine for their child is not always thinking of the consequences of that vaccination to other people. THese are markets in which subsidizing or regulating behavior can make everyone better off. Because the reason for requiring that a child be vaccinated before enrolling in school is not just to protect that child, because each child's vaccination affects others via potential contagions.

Robots take our jobs behavioral and economy influences
   Robot job behavior brings economy influences

If one day robots can replace human to do simple, even complex jobs. They will bring what influences to our global societial economy.The popular economic refrain declares that the

global middle class is dying and robots will soon take our jobs, e.g. shopping center customer service jobs, library service jobs, cinema ticket sale jobs, restaurant kitchen cooker jobs, even, bus drivers, taxi drivers etc. public transport driving jobs, accountant, doctors etc. professional jobs. Whether it is beautiful or petty matter if our future societies have many human jobs can be replaced to do from robots. Businessman must may reduce to employ employees and reduce to pay salary or wage, when robots can be replaced to do their employees tasks. But, societies must bring unemployement rate rises , due to societies will have many people loss jobs when their employers choose to buy robots to serve their clients or do any office tasks or customer service or cleaning etc. tasks.

In micro economy view, employers may save money in long term, but in macro economy view, it will cause unemployment ratio rises , even crime rate rises when there are many people lose

jobs in societies. These models of doom, though, fail to account for the hundreds of businesses riding the waves of change in their industries when robots may be invented to replace human to do many simple , even complex tasks in our future societies.

WE may image that one small factory needs to manufacture fishes canes to sell to supermarket, the small , cheaper stuff and higher margin parts of the fishes manufacture industry. Before, this factory needs to employe many human factory workers need to help every fresh customer makeing the perfect fishing gear, designed for performance, durability, and cost in order to achieve to manufacture every fish cane in whole fished processing manufacturing stages. Every worker needs to spend about 15 to twenty minutes to finish every fish cane , till to delivery to any supermarket to sell. If this fish canes manufacturing factory can apply manufacturing robots to help them to finish any one working tasks , every robot can only spend five minutes to finish whole fresh fish cane manufacturing process. Thus, every robot can help this factory save 10 to 15 minutes time to finsh every fish cane manufacturing process. IN fact, time is money, because when every robot can help this factory to reduce 10 to 15 minutes time to compare human worker. Then, this factory can finish about 20 fish canes in one hour if it can use robot to help it to manufacture fish canes. Otherwise, if this factory still use human workers to help it to manufacture fish canes, then it can finsh about 3 to 4 fish canes in one hour. SO, the manufacturing efficiency ensures that robots must help this fish manufacturing factory to raise fish canes number more than human workers. So, in robotic behavioral economy view, manufacturing robots must help this fish canes manufacturing factory to raise fish canes manufacturing number and deliver increasing number to supermarkets to prepare to sell every day. Robots can help this fish canes manufacturing factory bring manufacturing time saving, rising manufacturing efficiency, improving performance and reducing wages expenditure long time advantages in micro economy view. However, manufacturing robots can also bring disadvanages to society, e.g. increasing unemployment ratio, increasing crime rate,

this factory workers will lose jobs and income, they need earn social welfare from government and increasing government finance pressure in short time, even long time in macro economic view.

Stanford University graduate program in economics, Scott lecturer explained that "in demand and supply economic theory for robots supply and demand case, robots supply number increasing may influence human workers demand number decrease. It sometimes calls " the efficient frontier".

No specific human beings were mentioned in any of economics classes. As robots supply and demand in market case, They (robots) may be purely theoretical " agents" who reached to the most reasonable sale prices in order to persuade any one businessman buyer to make manufacturing robot buying decision whether robots can help him / her to bring how much saving time , saving money, saving cost, improving performance, efficiency economic benefit before he/she plans to reduce workers number when he/ she decides to apply robots to replace human workers in his/her factory or office or any service department, e.g. cinema ticket sale service, shopping center customer service, shopping center cleaning , supermarket customer service etc. service or sale tasks. When robots can replace human to do any one of these tasks in any organizations. So, robots may be human worker agents who reached to prices the way robots would react to a software command. There was nothing that explained why some people thrived and others did n't or why truly brilliant, hardworking people could fail when much lazier folks succeeded." Having been admitted to the Stanford University graduate program in economics, Scott lecturer hoped to get his answers there.

How robots influence our future social changing? Using the right technology can be a boon to your business in this economy. For internet example, it is easier than ever to find well-matched customers

all around the world, to stay in contact with them, and to more quickly design the products they want. If you focus solely on being cutting -edge, though you risk letting the technology take over what should be very robust relationships with your customers , employees, and colleagues. IN nowaddays society, technoligical advances and cutomation, personal

relationships in business are more crucial than ever. I mean that robots can not replace human to serve clients to let them to feel more comfortable and passion more easily. For shoe shop case example, if the shoe shop apply one robot to serve its clients to replace human shoe salesperson to serve its shoe customers. Robots ensure that they can not persuade every shoe potential buyer to make shoe buying decision more easily when robots need to contact every shoe potential buyer. The reason is simple, because robots can not touch any one shoe buyer individual emotion very easier.

If the shoe buyer needs the robots to help him/her to choose any right shoe styles when he/she can not feel himself / herself can make the most right shoe style choice decision. The robots can not replace human shoe salesperson to make shoe style choice judgement more easily. They must need longer time to analyze whether which shoe style may be the most suitable to the shoe buyer. Otherwise,human shoe salesperson may attempt to make the most right shoe style choice decision to help any one shoe buyer to chooce the most right style shoe because he/she owns shoe style sale experience, shoe style knowledge, the most important reason is that they can feel every shoe customer individual emotion to touch whether he/she will feel comfortable or happy when they attempt to help every shoe customer to seek the most right shoe style in every shoe customer whole shoe searching processing. Othwerwise, serving robots are only one machine, they can not touch or feel every shoe customer individual emotion whether he/she feel comfortable or unhappy or happy when they need to contact them in whole shoe searching processing. Hence, I believe that some tasks robots can not repalce human staff to do very easily. Otherwise, robots may bring disadvanatges to let any one businessman to loss his/her customers, due to robots can not touch every customer

emotion to compare human staff in service tasks more easily. Robots serving customer behaviors may cause money lose and customers number lose to the shop in micro economic view.

Intellectual human economic behaviors

What does intellectual human economic behaviors mean ? I believe that when we choose or decide to do intellectual behaviors, then our societies will be influenced to bring economic growth in consequence.I shall attempt to indicate pollution case to explain how and why eithet our intellectual or foolish behaviors may bring economic growth or recession in consequence as below:

On one hand, for air pollution social case aspect example, if we only consider to buy cars to drive for working aimr or holiday leisure aim. Then, our societies air will be polluted. Our health will be influenced to bad. Our car driving behaviors may cause global environment air pollution serously. In long tiem, global air pollution will bring our bodies health to be bad. Although, ourselves car driving behaviors may bring our driving travelling leisure enjoyment and comfortable feeling in short time, also we so not need to pay public transport fare often, but we need to compensate ourselves health economic intangible loss due to air pollution , when cars number increases, dirty air will cause ouselves health to become bad.

In the result, we will need to pay more medical expenditure when we are old age, due to ourselves bodies will become bad, due to we breathe global dirty air every day, due to ourselves cars pollute air in long time, e.g. 10 to 20 years, even 30 more without limited air pollution environment. So, driving cars behavior may be one kind of human foolish behavior and our foolish behavior may bring ourselves future long time medical expenditure absolutely.

One the other hand, water pollution social aspect, if we often keep much rubblish to pollute sea, oil exploration porcessing pollute ocean , ships gas pollute ocaen, then fishes will eat polluted food and drive dirty water, due to global ocean is polluted.

In fact, because human only to conside how to buy boats to carry on leisure enjoyment activities, or catch cruises to travel on the sea. Also, oil manufacturers only consider researching anywhere to find new oil exploration places to manufacture oil product, when their oil exploration processes pollute ocarn . Consequently, global fishes drink polluted warer or eat polluted food. They will have poison. SO, human will have high chance to eat poison polluted fishes, due to fishes are poison or are polluted.

So, human is doing foolish activities, we only hope to find oil exploration places to pollute ocean or we only spend money to buy ticket to catch ships to travel anywhere in global ocean. All of these human foolish behaviors will bring pollution to global ocean. On consequently, we will need to compensate to eat polluted or dirty or poision fishes, ourselves bodies health will be bad. In long time, we need have high chance to pay medical expenditure when we are old. So, pollution case may be one good example to explain how and why human foolish behavior may influence ourselves future need to compensate serious medical loss.

All of these human foolish behavior will bring pollution to global ocean. On consequently, we will need to compensate to eat polluted or dirty or poison fished , ourselves bodies health will be bad. In long time, we will have high chance to pay medical expenditure, when we are old. So, pollution case may be one good example to explain how and why human ourselves intellectual or foolish behaviors may influence future long time economic loss or economic growth or recession in micro and micro economic view.

On another water pollution aspect hand, if we often keep rubbish to sea, oil exploration processing pollutes ocean and ships' gas pollute ocean, then fishes will eat polluted food and drink dirty water, due to fishes will eat polluted food and drink dirty sea water because the global ocean is polluted seriously.

In fact, because human only consider how to buy boats to carry on any leisure water activities, or catches cruises to travel on the sea. Also, oil manufacturers only consider any where to find oil exploratin places to manufacture oil products from ocean, when their pol exploration processes can plooute ocean. Consequently, global fishes drink polluted water or eat direty food. They will have poison. So, human will have high chance to eat poison fishes.

Otherwise, such as pollution case, it can infuence inflation or deflation. Consequently, the reason indicates supply and demand theory. If air pollution is serious, then we will consider health issue, global cars demand number may be influenced to reduce, when global cars number demand will reduce, global car prices and supply number will need to change to fall down in order to attract or persuade global car consumers choose to make car purchase decision.

Hence, global car manufacture number and car price will be influenced to reduce, due to global air pollution issue. Consequently, deflation will occur because when the country citizen usually does not spend much extra saving money to buy car expensive goods. Money value will be low. Otherwise, if global cair pollution is not serious, human considers to buy cars to enjoy driving leisure lives. So, global car demand is influenced to increase , also global car price will also influenced to increase.

Consequently, gobal human will choose to buy cars to drive. Due to we accept to spend extra saving to buy expensive car goods. Car sale price and supply may be influenced to rise up. Money value is influenced to reduce. Inflation may be influenced, due to global car consumers number increases, we would not have extra money to spend easily. Car expensive goods expenditure influences our spending habit to avoid to make car purchase decision more easily. So, human intellectual or foolish activities may bring inflation or deflation consequency in possible indirectly in macro economic view.

On conclusion, above pollution case explain that how and why human intellectual or foolish economic behaviors may bring inflation or deflation consequency as wll as economic growth or recession consequency as well as any goods demand and supply increasing or decreasing consequency. It implies that human behavior may have indirect relationship to influence any goods demand and supply number to either increase or decrease result as well as any goods price will be influenced to increase or decrease in micro and macro economic view.